VULNERABLE TO THE HOLY

For Ronan

Vulnerable to the Holy
in faith, morality and art

Enda McDonagh

the columba press

First published in 2004 by
the columba press
55A Spruce Avenue, Stillorgan Industrial Park,
Blackrock, Co Dublin

Cover by Bill Bolger
Front cover: *St Kevin and the Blackbird* by Imogen Stuart
Back cover: *The Windhover searches the winter* by Tony O'Malley
Origination by The Columba Press
Printed in Ireland by ColourBooks Ltd, Dublin

ISBN 1 85607 460 9

Acknowledgements

A number of the chapters here have appeared in issues of *The Furrow*, in *Irish Pages*, *The Irish Times* and in various publications abroad.

The cover illustrations are reproduced by kind permission of Imogen Stuart and Jane O'Malley. The picture on page 180 is from *L'opera grafica di Pietro Parigi* published by Città di Vita Edizioni.

'St Kevin and the Blackbird' by Seamus Heaney is reproduced by kind permission of Faber and Faber. 'Advent' by Patrick Kavanagh is printed by kind permission of the Trustees of the Estate of the late Katherine B. Kavanagh, through the Jonathan Williams Literary Agency.

Table of Contents

Introduction

This, it must be said, is not the book I intended to write on my retirement so many years ago. But that might happen to real writers too and not just to theological scribblers. And retirement from full-time teaching turned out to be quite different from the expected quiet days of lots of reading and a little writing. At one stage I sought refuge in Glenstal Abbey from what I could only term 'the rat-race of retirement'. For some time before that I had promised myself a book about ultimate questions which I had provisionally entitled *The Risk of God*. A certain amount of reading, talking and even writing developed around this theme, enough to keep the possibility alive, but not nearly enough to form the basis for any substantial publication. Retirement had too many other calls and writing became less easy than I had hoped. Most of the calls were worthy and the work and words they demanded began to form a theme of their own which eventually I learned to call, *Vulnerable to the Holy*. The people, occasions and organisations from which the calls came found me vulnerable to their claims because I believed they were somehow in their claims mediators of the holy. This does not make me holy in any recognisable sense. The holiness was all theirs or their God's. But it did alert me to the holiness embodied in such contingent beings and occasions and how it could be accessible to the least pious of us in our prosaic attending to their requests and needs.

For much of my theological life I had been conscious of the connection between otherness and holiness, deriving scripturally and perhaps philosophically from the idea of God as the ultimate other. I had also been aware of the negative connotations of other in personal, social and cultural contexts. The others were strangers, aliens, threatening, inferior, the enemy in so many situations of discrimination, exclusion and oppression. Settled and traveller, nationalist and unionist, Catholic and

Protestant, Irish and British were in the tiny island of Ireland caught in the antagonism of the alienated. In the wider world there were and are endless examples of personal and structural differences plotted along a hostile graph of mutual estrangement and conflict. Not much of the holy and enriching stranger in evidence in that world. Yet that is the world of the God of the whole human race called to mutual loving, peace and fulfillment. And it is their own very otherness as male and female, as belonging to diverse races, cultures and religions that mediates the ultimate otherness of their God and provides the basis for their mutual sanctification rather than the mutual degradation in which they so often engage.

In this volume a series of exploratory probes into areas in which the author has been engaged intellectually, emotionally and practically over seven or eight years, have been assembled as direct or indirect illustrations of how the other may be primarily holy-making if one accepts the grace of openness and vulnerability. The fuller explanation of what vulnerability to the other as holy means is offered in Chapter I, the last chapter to be written as the reader might imagine. The following chapters are divided into four parts, dealing with some of the main preoccupations of the author over these years and his attempts to explore them in their strangeness, threatening or promising as the case might be. The Catholic Church as the home church receives extensive consideration in the first of these parts, numbered two here. These chapters were written at different times for different occasions and publications but they share at least in hope a sense of the strange richness and poverty of the church today. They may also offer some useful suggestions about how in its people, leaders and structures it can be vulnerable to the holiness of the wider church and world and render them in turn vulnerable to the holiness, which for all its deformities, the church continues to bear and to bear witness to.

The next part (III) focuses on the moral issues which have been of particular theological and pastoral concern in recent times. As a theologian whose professional work has been predominantly concerned with morality for Christians, although I hesitate over the term moral theologian, I have been called to speak and write on many of these issues. In that context I first discovered the significance of the other for morality and ethics courtesy of such thinkers as Emmanuel Levinas. One could combine that with the scriptural connection between otherness (*qadosh*) and holiness and with an increasing awareness of the moral life as the expression of grace or the indwelling of the Holy Spirit (the *lex nova* of St Thomas Aquinas) rather than obedience to legal prescriptions. Then it was easier to see how holiness and morality together involved both openness/vulnerability to the neighbour and to God. In the central areas of Christian living discussed here, from the very personal of friendship, sexuality and marriage to the great contemporary social issues of HIV and AIDS and of peace and war, openness and vulnerability to the others is crucial, cruciform and Christian.

In part IV another strand of life and otherness predominates. For some people, some of them close friends, ethics, aesthetics and Christian faith are natural companions. For many others they are not. A slow learner in this, as in many other dimensions of living, I gradually became vulnerable to the otherness in beauty of a wide range of artistic objects. Poetry and literature came easier and had a childhood background. Other art forms came later, some much later. And then there was the grace of friends, art lovers and even artists, so that one's lack of formal education ceased to matter. As poems and plays, paintings and sculptures began to take one over at least temporarily, vulnerability to a deeper beauty and otherness became manifest. Not that one might use the artefact as a means to something else even God anymore than one should use another human being as such a means. No, the poem or painting had to be appreciated (and re-appreciated) in itself, in its integrity, in its distinctive otherness and beauty and so one rested there. Yet the experience of all that created otherness might well spark a sense of something beyond, in the Christian art lover a sense of the Creator God without in any way belittling the creative human and her creativity. All this is perhaps easier to experience than to describe. Further attempts to describe the creative work of the artist may also open one to new awareness of the divine working of creation. While the sensitivity may be expanded, the mystery of divine and even of human creativity remains.

The shorter part V on the vulnerable self recognises more explicitly what has been implied throughout, that the self is also an other even to the self. In a profession which mostly evades personal exposure, in writing these chapters the theologian lets down the guard in a more intimate but still limited way. Yet the exploration of vulnerability, otherness and holiness would be more incomplete without some such personal exposure. And no commentary is really necessary.

PART ONE

Vulnerable to the Holy

CHAPTER ONE

Encountering the Other

To walk abroad in the sanctities of all our days is not to be unaware of their horrors. Nor is it to refuse the challenge of these horrors, from famine to HIV/AIDS to the cluster-bombing of women and children. The horrors themselves may indeed be a way of making us vulnerable to the holy. But they are not the only way or indeed the primary way. A baby's first word may be more piercing than its first cry of pain, the first crocus than the fading rose, the Manhattan skyline than the Ground Zero gap. Every body, every where and every when bear the features of beauty and destruction, their double capacity to render us vulnerable to the holy. The holy, the Holy One, the Holy Spirit, the God of creation, redemption and resurrection is all present, all piercing, all healing. Openness to that presence is gift and call, at once costing and fulfilling not less than everything.

Letting be
'And God said: Let there be ... And God saw that it was good.' In chapter one of the Book of Genesis the author provides a sense of the dramatic tension of the various stages of creation and of their divine resolution. Chapter three reveals the deeper drama of light and darkness, of good and evil involved in the confrontation between a divine authority and human freedom, requiring a new, prolonged, painful but finally redemptive 'Let there be' by the creator turned redeemer God. The creative and saving Word of God, the divine let there be, has always also enjoyed human forms. 'In the image of God, (God) created (humanity).' 'And the (divine) Word was made (human) flesh' in Jesus Christ with human consent. 'Be it done unto me according to thy Word.' Human letting be was doubly endorsed in the mystery of redemptive incarnation.

In daily human interchange the mysterious divine concentrate is both concealed and revealed. The passive and active let-

ting be of all our tribe in accepting and enabling reflects the re-
demptive-creative work of God; it opens us to the holy in other
human beings and in all creation. It allows us to see that they are
good as of God and of the light, however much they may also be
of the darkness, just like ourselves. Discovering and enacting the
complex demands of passive and active letting be is a lifelong
task for human beings just as it is a creation-long commitment of
their Creator. Along that road of discovering and enacting lies
human fulfilment (or holiness).

Passive letting be could well be misinterpreted as mere toler-
ance or even indifference. Based on the divine model, it should
rather signal patient and loving recognition and acceptance of
the different, of the other. It is in that loving recognition and acceptance of the other that one first becomes vulnerable to the
holy. The neatly deflating comment, 'It takes a saint to live with
one', might be expanded to embrace in a positive way the whole
range of human relationships and encounters. All human to-
getherness has the potential to be sanctifying as each renders the
other vulnerable to the holy. The holiness of the human other,
however disguised or distorted, provides the basis for each person's opening to the sanctifying presence of the human and so of
the ultimate other. The seventy times seven forgiveness of Jesus'
counsel is rooted in this presence and power of the ultimate
other as mediated by the human other. 'It makes a saint to live
with one other human being.'

In the moral letting be of human relationships the passive or
accepting is primary. Acceptance of the other person as there, as
she is in her otherness, is fundamental. Of couse it is never and
can never be sheer passivity. The acceptance and respect for
other as other calls for multiple if only tiny active responses, a
smile of recognition or a scowl of rejection, a seat on a bus for an
older passenger, letting somebody through the door first. The elements of interpersonal politeness are the enactment of that
recognition and acceptance of the other person as an other, as
equally and fully person. The decline of many of these conven-
tions may be no more than a passing phase, particularly in
younger bustling people; it may also be a symptom of declining
respect for people, particularly the elderly or the otherwise limited in physical or mental energy and social aggression. Family,
friendship and professional caring provide at their best the
models for these accepting and enabling, creative and enduring

relationships which give any society its cohesion, warmth and vibrancy. Passive and active letting be combine in justice and freedom for the other, in fulfilment and peace for the community; at least they have the basis for doing so.

Letting be, active and passive, is not just a matter of human relationships, of enabling other human beings to come into existence, of accepting, respecting and actively helping them to develop. It applies to the much wider worlds in which humans have their being. The most obvious of these is the natural world with its othernesses offering human beings beauty and sustenance and at the same time demanding recognition and respect. Letting the world of nature be in the passive and active senses translates into a self-conscious environmental ethics for humanity today in a number of different ways. The more widespread of these ethics is predominantly utilitarian. The earth and its resources including its climate must be increasingly cared for, for humanity's sake, as useful to the quality of life and eventually necessary to the survival of the human race. There may be scientific dispute about the empirical evidence for the extent of the damage which a greedy and uncaring populace inflicts daily on the planet and on how many species are destroyed and when, and still more about technology's ability to repair or replace these lost resources. There is little dispute that real damage to human living also results from continuing human disrespect for and abuse of the planet. Such self-centred fears and utilitarian considerations may well be the beginning of environmental wisdom, of letting the planet be, passively and actively.

At another level of argument, respect for the natural environment dwells on the sheer givenness of it, its wonder and beauty. Let the world be in all its glory might seem to be the implicit cry. The argument is not narrowly aesthetic but would seem to see a close connection between aesthetic appreciation of what's there and the ethical human response to it as first of all thanksgiving and praise. Such response would clearly exclude selfish, primarily commercial exploitation and simple abuse. It would seem at the same time to permit and encourage the kind of technological and other human development which respects the grain of the universe and is necessary to human fulfilment. Recent writings by George Monbiot and George Steiner ('Humans as guests of creation') seem to adopt this approach as more true to human responsibility and more persuasive than sheer utilitarianism.

For Christians and other believers in a divine Creator and creation, the 'aesthetic/ethical' approach has much to offer. Blamed, as they have sometimes been, for the disenchantment of nature and so leaving it open to technological exploitation, Christians have a duty to recover their sense of nature as God's loving gift, their appreciation of its beauty and their own role as stewards of that nature as God's gift and call to them. A good deal of theological-scientific dialogue has occurred in recent decades in the various Christian churches and in other faith-communities. Such analysis with some follow-up practice has occurred at many levels in the churches from the Vatican out. In Ireland individual thinkers and activists like John O'Donohue and Sean McDonagh have provided aesthetic, ethical and religious leadership in this area. So have many groups from the Green Party to local community groups intent on saving particular beautiful landscapes, bogscapes, rivers, lakes and seashore. At the international level, organisations like Trócaire with its series on 'Christian Perspectives on Development' are tackling environmental problems in the poorer countries of the south.

In an effort to drive home the urgency of the environmental task, some writers propose equal recognition for all living species and regard any departure from this, particularly by giving a privileged position to the human species, as unethical. The lording over all other species and disregard for their existence and value, for their contribution to the wonder of the world and for their capacities, including the capacity to suffer pain, is certainly unethical on the part of human beings. The insistence that human beings belong within the natural world is important but the denial of a discontinuity as well as a continuity with that world seems contrary to maintaining human ethical responsibilities to the rest of the natural world. How far these responsibilities extend is often very difficult to determine. Animals and birds for example might seem to enjoy a certain priority. Their care for their young as well as their mating habits are often admirable in themselves but can they be described as ethical and the subject of rights in the senses applicable to humans? Perhaps these debates are ultimately irresolvable and unnecessary if human beings live up to their own ethical responsibilities as stewards rather than masters.

As far as this essay is concerned, human otherness and that of the rest of the natural world demands a recognition and respect which ultimately rests in its rootedness in God and God's continuing creative activity, the divine letting be in which humans are invited and empowered to partake. This human letting be, in its accepting and enabling senses, renders each human vulnerable to the holy, to the immediate sacredness of every human being, including the self as other, and to the sacred character of the universe itself as created by, reflecting and even participating in the holiness of God.

Letting go
Letting be, in both its active and passive senses of enabling and accepting the other, demands for its completion a letting go. In the passive sense suggested by this metaphor in the first place, the other human being, to take an easy example, has to be let live her own distinctive life. This should not mean abandonment of or indifference to the other but a caring and supportive respect for the other's freedom and privacy. Parents often learn this the hard way. Vulnerability to the other human being may take a very painful form as children grow up and grow away from their parents, pain already anticipated in the process of giving birth. Retaining the child in the womb, refusing to let go in that elementary sense is not a viable option or a serious temptation for a developing mother but there may be later temptations for either or both parents to become possessive of a child and refuse to let it go into the wider world in which it has to mature. A spouse or partner might also become possessive of the other in jealous and destructive ways. Such destructive possessiveness extends to the whole range of human relationships with other humans but also with non-human animate and inanimate objects. And in a paradoxical and ultimately tragic way, a person's possessiveness translates into that person being possessed and so enslaved by her possessions in money or property or even in family or other human love. The ability to let go in a positive and respecting fashion is essential to personal freedom and security.

This may be more important but also more difficult where the other person has deeply insulted or offended the self, the self's family or property. Harbouring grudges is a human weakness which may become a destructive obsession. The letting go which is necessary to the grudge-bearer's liberation is finally a form of forgiveness. Loving one's enemies is the great human letting go, all the more painful of course but no less necessary where the move is not reciprocated. It is the loving attention to the other as other, to the holy in the enemy, that releases the loving one from the fear of that other and renders the loving one vulnerable to the holy in opponent or enemy.

For a range of physical, emotional and even spiritual reasons one's self may be the hated other. Low self-esteem and self-loathing are frequently mentioned as sources of personal unhappiness. 'I can never forgive myself for such and such' is not an uncommon attitude. Perceived or imagined personal threats, flaws or failures can restrict normal living and relationships to the point of neurosis, mental breakdown or even suicide, a far too frequent tragedy in Ireland today for whatever reasons. A recovery of the sense of self as valuable and lovable will not be achieved by sheer concentration on the self, which intensifies the vicious circle. In the circle of loving others, including the still troubled self as other, the value, the unique otherness of the self, its holiness can be restored. The self also must be continually renewed in its openness to its own holy otherness, in Christian terms to its mediation of the ultimate otherness of its creator and healer God.

Letting go has much broader application and much deeper roots than the purely person-to-person or person-to-object relations discussed above, although such relationships provide obvious illustrations of the need to let go, of the temptations to resist, and of the pain and the consequence of accepting or resisting. In the political sphere letting be and letting go assume their own form, encounter their own needs and their own temptations.

Letting be as enabling people to realise their full potential as human beings and citizens is the first and most important task in politics. What that full potential might be and how it might be realised will vary from polity to polity and from era to era. In the present era, with its opposing dynamics of globalisation and fragmentation, political leaders in the national, regional and global arenas face daunting tasks. At the most basic levels people must be helped simply to live in contexts of war and terror, of famine, drought and kindred natural disasters, of HIV-AIDS and similar plagues. This is the global political situation which the dominantly economic globalisation at work at present is exacerbating rather than relieving. Despite the rhetoric and the promises from the Millennium Development Goals at the UN summit in 2000 to the Dublin Declaration on HIV-AIDS in 2004, action is so slow, inadequate and uncoordinated that the 'letting go', which might have been liberation from much of their enslavement for many of these peoples, has become abandonment of them to their continuing suffering and premature dying.

Such abandonment of the powerless by the powerful has complex roots. The temptations of profit, power and pleasure obscure the human needs of others, their innate dignity and its accompanying rights, their sacredness and holiness as persons. Ethnic and racial differences, religion, culture and gender compound the power-games and prevent the kind of vulnerability to the stigmatised others which could be liberating for both sides. One of the 'holy' figures of twentieth-century politics, holy in his sensitivity to the enemy-other, the Mahatma Gandhi spoke of the emancipation needed by the British as well as by the Indian people. Exploitative power in whatever arena, political, economic, military, religious, gender or race, is eventually enslaving of master as well as subject. Letting go of such power in the process of enabling or letting be, of liberating and letting go the people subject to it, is the way to liberation and fulfilment of the people with power. All that is very difficult to perceive and very painful to effect. To refuse that voluntary letting be and letting go of the oppressed is to face recurring insecurity and eventually loss of the power itself and frequently to a new and powerful antagonist. Empires are in the end self-destructive although their history of 'other-destruction' until that end occurs, usually makes very sad reading.

Letting be and letting go are aptly illustrated in the work of artists. The painful labour whereby a writer or other artist brings a work into existence, enables it to be, can lead to the pain of deciding when the work is finished, and when it may be offered to publisher or public, when its creator will let it go. For some artists and some work these decisions may prove impossible so the artist is trapped by the unfinished or unfinishable work and the public deprived of the pleasure of it. Acceptance of the work with its flaws and in its otherness means letting it go so that it is no longer simply under the artist's control, but in a strange world where its reception may offer reassuring encouragement or dispiriting discouragement. In the releasing as in the making, the joy and the pain will be mixed but both may contribute to the growth of the artist and the enrichment of her society.

Letting God

For the religious believer and community the letting be and letting go in religious terms follow similar patterns to those outlined earlier. The stakes, however, are higher. The holy to whom the religious believer is vulnerable is named as God, the ultimate Other, and the context is that of recognising one's ultimate origin and achieving one's ultimate destiny. Such stakes and such a context do not annul the reality and value of letting be and letting go in person-to-person contexts, in the political and environmental contexts or in the artistic and cultural contexts. The higher stakes and final context confirm, transfigure and in the end transcend all these. Letting be and letting go in every sphere of life reach their culmination in letting God.

In the creation story of Genesis, God is not only letting be, as we saw, but also letting go. This is the risk of creation for God, introducing into being other reality distinct from Godself. As the Genesis account goes, God rejoiced in this otherness as gift but as the story proceeds the gift turned threat, alien to and alienated from God in its climactic creatures, man and woman. This was an offence to God's own holiness, the divine otherness as mirrored particularly in the human, and indeed to the holiness of the whole universe as it was alienated from its human stewards (Gen 3). In halting human terms one might speak of a divine temptation to undo the divine handiwork and wipe out creation in order to restore the previous pristine holiness. At various times in the history of humanity, and of Israel according to biblical sources, this threat was proclaimed unless the people repented and turned again to their one Creator and Lord, Yahweh. And by these accounts it became a near reality with Noah and the Flood. All this, while primarily directed at human return to its original blessedness, its true otherness to God, signals perhaps a need on the part of God to have the divine creative otherness or holiness fully efficacious in the world. God's holiness is restricted by human selfishness and sinfulness. Hence the divine promises made known to Moses and the prophets, of a promised land of milk and honey, of a new covenant of the heart, with the dry bones of a dead creation to be brought alive again and, most mysteriously of all, this to be accomplished by a suffering and servant Messiah rather than by a thunderous intervention of the Lord of Hosts.

In pursuit of the true otherness of humanity and the universe,

God entered that cosmic and human otherness, became human in Jesus Christ. This letting go by God of God in incarnation transcends all human imagining and yet seems itself transcended in the surrender unto death on a cross by the Son of God made man. It is in that dying into resurrection and the sending of the Spirit, which completes the divine letting be of creation and the divine letting go of incarnation by letting God, by letting God be God in God's trinitarian self and in God's universe. Jesus' insight about the seed falling into the ground and that whoever would save his life must surrender it, seems to apply to the Creator no less than to the creature.

As it applies to the human creature in the thousand cuts and losses of her mortal life, it prepares her for the final letting be, letting go and letting God of her own death. At that last vulnerable time the holiness of the others she has encountered, human and cosmic, poetic and prosaic, and the holiness of the self which has been blessed by them and by her God, may face in hope and in peace, if not yet free of all anxiety, the ultimate creative, forgiving and sanctifying Other.

PART TWO

In the Community of Faith

CHAPTER TWO

Shared Despair?

As the sea rises higher yet the time for diplomatic niceties is past. Only plain blunt speech can help now. Risks of giving offence to the 'strong' must be taken. Above all some serious attempt must be made to get below the surface of the attitudes and exchanges which have dominated this Easter crisis so far.

The most glaring absence amongst the guests invited to address the Extraordinary Meeting of the Irish Bishops' Conference on Monday 8 April 2002 was any representative of the abused and their families. For all the organisational excuses which might be advanced, the absence emphasised once more the bishops' public image as a body which operates in secret with the occasional professional advisor. It contrasted powerfully with a meeting the previous week between the Minister for Health and representatives of the survivors' group and the rapid announcement of the appointment of George Bermingham SC, to consult with all parties concerned and make recommendations within three months to the government on what kind of civil inquiry should be held into events in the Diocese of Fems. The presence of one agitated protesting survivor of child sex abuse, Gerry Kelly, provided some unusual dramatics at Maynooth. Despite the calming encounter with Bishop Willie Walsh and Kelly's later reception by Archbishop Brady and Cardinal Connell, the underlying weakness of episcopal engagement emerged once more. The announcement of an independent internal audit of how the dioceses were implementing the 1996 *Guidelines on Clerical Sex Abuse* without name, terms of reference or time-scale, did not really assuage the anger and fear which have so deeply affected the victims, or the much wider body of committed Catholic people and priests. However, together with the promise to extend the remit of the Bishops' Child Protection Office (in unspecified ways at an unspecified time) and the appointment of Judge Gillian Hussey to chair the Bishops' Child

Protection Committee were further signs of a beginning to grapple with the problems, weak though the signs maybe.

Lest this summary of such recent events seem unfair to the Irish Catholic Church and bishops (with one of their own hitting them when they are down), it has to be remembered how long these problems with sex abuse and other failures of church leadership have been publicly known and commented on. From the 1983 Abortion Referendum to that of 2002, many committed theologians and other Catholic commentators have commented on the ill-advised manner in which the episcopal leadership sought to devise and promote policies without any participation by those who would have had reasonable and faith-based reservations about the courses to be pursued. The self-enclosing meeting of the bishops at Maynooth or elsewhere seemed too often to result in a policy determined by the most conservative common denominator. When it did not, some of the more conservative broke ranks. To compound the self-enclosing consultations, individual bishops took it upon themselves to be more isolationist still. Only Bishop Willie Walsh took advantage of such freedom to voice a more open and Christian view, all the more credible because of his pastoral sensitivity, heightened undoubtedly by his pastoral pilgrimage some years ago from the south-westem end of his diocese in Clare to the far north-eastem end in Tipperary.

Several very potent opportunities occurred in these last years when the Irish Bishops' Conference might have broken out of their isolation. The first very significant one was the resignation of Bishop Casey and the associated scandal. (Not that Bishop Casey's lapse should be put on the same level as sexual abuse of the young.) The whole country was shocked at first, many were subsequently sympathetic, but most accepted the need for serious reform in the style of bishoping and in the manner of episcopal appointment. It was undoubtedly an opportunity for reflection and reform involving the whole church, lay, religious, priests and bishops. Sensing the atmosphere and spotting the opportunity, the late Bishop Michael Murphy of Cork suggested about this time some kind of pastoral synod or assembly of the whole Irish church to analyse the situation and develop strategies of response. This suggestion was taken seriously by the National Council of Irish Priests at their Annual General Conference in 1995 and brave efforts were made to promote the idea and the development of a five-year preparatory phase at parochial, diocesan and regional level. There was no evidence of episcopal support and the idea gradually faded, although various parishes and dioceses have had assemblies and listening days, with assembly days too often confined to priests. Yet there is material for development there, given the imagination and the will.

The Brendan Smith crisis created much deeper shock waves than the Casey affair. Given the all-Ireland range of his abusing and the political crisis about his extradition, a radical response from the church leaders might be expected. Soothing and sometimes evasive words let the opportunity dribble away and the complacent routines were resumed.

And so it went until the BBC programme on *Sueing the Pope* hit the people. Bishops first scrambled for cover ('all protocols followed in my diocese', 'no knowledge of situation in Ferns'). Very slowly they began to recognise the shame and the anger afflicting a national audience much wider than the frustrated victims who had struggled for so long to get their story heard.

And where are we now, the community of Irish believers, the Irish church? Still largely excluded from the process of coming to grips with the darkness which overshadows every one of us in our faith, hope and love. Will the darkness that overshadows become a darkness that overwhelms, robbing us of our faith and love and above all of our hope? Are we destined for despair, for the despair which has dogged these victims for decades, as they sought a loving, pastoral hand to accompany them through their darkness. That's where we all need to be now, as brothers and sisters in Christ, trying to share the pain and the darkness and the despair. Of course we may not impose ourselves and we may not for many who have suffered so much be welcome companions at this time. But seeking to be companions in pain and frustration and despair is our first call.

It is also the first call of our leaders, the bishops. Without consistent and continuing sharing and companionship with the suffering, and at this particular time with those who have suffered sex abuse at the hands of their representatives, they will never develop the sensibility and creativity necessary to take us all beyond despair.

Before 'beyond' comes 'within', the immersion in the pain of the others, the sharing. People in protected positions like bishops or even priests and a range of others, find it very difficult personally and structurally to hear and share the pain of victims, their sense of near, indeed real despair. The long struggle of the haemophiliacs infected with Hepatitis C or HIV through contaminated blood products has been a very painful episode in Irish history which too many people in protected positions evaded or resisted for too long. At a much lower level but in a church context, the frustrations and pain endured by many dedicated lay people working in Irish church commissions on the episcopal decision to move them all to Maynooth was never thought to be shared by the bishops, even now when such a high percentage of one agency and some at the highest level are leaving. The consoling words they received from some priests, 'that's just how we are treated', only increases the tendency to despair of church if not of God.

Bishops need to come much closer to the victims of church structures and bureaucracy if they are to learn the depth of their suffering. This will require time and skills. Are there any courses in pastoral skills for bishops old, new or would-be? Without sharing the pain and hopelessness of the victims they will never adequately respond to them. And the pain to be experienced must be that of the others and not the self-referential or self-indulgent pain too often voiced by authorities in face of criticism.

As that sharing in the darkness and despair grows, church leaders and all of us may be led to the Spirit beyond Calvary to some resurrection hope and insight. One Irish insight might be that humility is only painfully gained through humiliation. Easy predictions of a humbler church during past crises only increased the disillusionment. The humiliation of the victims must open all to sharing the humiliation of losing power, prestige and protection. That is why even now opening up the protective enclosures of bishops' meetings and houses to broadly representative groups geared to particular occasions, would begin the process of sharing the joys and sorrows, the hopes and despairs of our Catholic people. This will itself be a painful process. The powerful do not shed or even share power easily: the powerless do not assume or even share it easily. But these should be pains of growth, unlike the present widespread pains of decline. A further move in the liberation from the church's paralysing power structures will be its full co-operation with the Bermingham and subsequent State inquiry. Pedantic debates about files and records and information will not presumably prevent full disclosure. The further pain of that full disclosure will be alleviated more effectively by the involvement of victims, people and priests in analysing the data and preparing strategies of response.

If sharing the despair of the victims could really provoke the episcopal clerical church into surrendering its power and privileges in a genuinely interdependent and participative church, hope would gradually be restored and healing would really begin. May God grant it be so.

CHAPTER THREE

The Crisis of Governance

In most theological discussions, language and its associates, image and concept, are subject to distressing complexity and confusion. Theological debates share these difficulties with most serious human debates but they have their own particular intensification as human language wrestles with divine mysteries.

The plurality of ways in which we speak of church and church governance has its roots in the Bible, particularly the New Testament. However, a subsequent tangled history added immensely to the complexity and hence the ambiguity in ways which the pastoral inclusiveness and theological power of Vatican II could not wholly dissipate. Indeed if we are to be faithful to the tradition and authentically contemporary in our discussions, we will have to accept the limitations and possibilities of plurality and ambiguity.

The primacy and the ultimacy of God
As language about God and about everything else in relation to God (Aquinas), theology has a singular starting and finishing point. This does not mean that the explicit first and last words in any piece of theological analysis or reflection must be the name God or its equivalent. It does mean that the presupposition of such discussion and its final point of reference is in Christian theology the God of Jesus Christ. So a theology of the church or its governance cannot be carried on in any self-enclosing way as if it were not to be finally open to and judged by the presence and character of God as manifest in Jesus Christ.

The priority of the believing people
Lumen Gentium's reversal of the hitherto prevailing church order of a hierarchy and clergy with a people attached, to a people with a hierarchical structure internal to itself, has not seriously affected the image or reality of the church for baptised or or-

dained. The document itself, reflecting divisions among the Council fathers, is not entirely clear. An inevitable ambiguity persists which allows the conflicting interpretations which can readily translate into power struggles and accusations of bad faith or at least of mistaken reading of Vatican II. Here the more general Council principle headlined above, the fuller Christian tradition into which all particular documents must be fitted, and the first and final point of reference, the manifestation of God in Jesus Christ will slowly, painfully and prayerfully lead to truer insight and greater Christian agreement.

Experience of church

Plurality and ambiguity are nowhere more rampant than in the experience of church, whether considered historically or contemporaneously, be it that of particular groups such as bishops, priests or lay people, or that of particular individuals within these groups or even that of a particular stage in the life of that individual or group. Most of us have had quite different experiences of church in the course of our lives although we may feel that we could generalise about it as a whole in a coherent enough way. To complicate matters further, there may be real disagreement about what counts as experience of church. It was and is quite common to explain to somebody who has been hurt by a particular priest or bishop that that individual should not be confused with the church, so their experience of hurt was not an experience of church at all. Related to this is the statement denying that the church itself is sinful although it is composed of sinners. Without the opportunity or indeed capacity to examine all these dimensions of experience of church, it is important to stress the diversity of this experience, the distinction between what might be described as the church of empirical experience and the church of faith idealisation (the sinless church) and the obligation of different members and groups of members to share experience of church in both conversation and experiment.

Pilgrims in communion

Two descriptions/models/images of church which are currently very influential, that of the church as pilgrim people and that of the church as communion, are helpful in illuminating the difficulties of experience of church and in tackling issues of governance. The pilgrim people suggests a dynamic open group moving towards a future still largely unknown. Movement rather than order, equality and mutuality in comradeship rather than status and superiority, inferiority, and functions in response to needs rather than set offices, are some of the characteristics of people on pilgrimage according to Victor Turner in his classic study. Communion at first sight suggests a more ordered and static group with certain resonances of hierarchy and exclusion. These seem to receive further confirmation in relating the communion of the church, as one should, to the eucharist with its presiding superior and powers of exclusion. The ambiguities of both these models are obvious. (Pilgrim peoples from Israel to New England to Lourdes readily develop hierarchy and exclusivity also.)

At deeper theological levels and at practical levels, pilgrimage and communion have much to offer in understanding and living governance in the church. Where pilgrimage is seen as characteristic of humanity as well as of church, its further created depth is revealed. Church cannot escape this created historical moving character which it needs to manifest and realise in its life and structures. The dynamism, the equality and mutuality, the functions in response to needs, will have to be renewed again and again among the whole pilgrim people liable through laziness or insecurity to seek refuge from reality in an apparently fixed order. At the other extreme, the group might become simply chaotic. To continue on pilgrimage the pilgrims need to be organised and sustained by thoughtful and caring leaders. In the experience of pilgrimage closer bonds of community are formed. The deeper reality of communion becomes possible if provisional and always a community that is already and not yet, the heavenly dimension of the earthly church partially realised. The Eastern and Western emphases in the understanding of church and eucharist are implicit here, expressed together in the common phrase 'communion of saints'. It is the expression in time of the etemal communion of the Trinity, in itself of course constituted by the dynamic and mutual loving of the three different but equally divine persons. Pilgrimage and communion then belong together as reinforcing yet mutually correcting models. To renew life and mutuality in what can be a juridicised, static and oppressive community/communion model, more explicit realisation of the pilgrim model is required. This might be helped, for example, by deliberate 'pilgrim Sundays' in parishes

and dioceses where all status and privileges were set aside and
people came together dressed only in their 'baptismal garments'
as equal members of the pilgrim people, with equal concern and
responsibility for charting the course ahead.

The church, local and global, particular and universal
Both models of pilgrim people and communion, as well as other
models of church, have to take account of the peculiar unity in
diversity which characterises the church and its governance.
This is more complex than the many simple models of 'local'
and 'universal' might suggest, as it has to take into account not
merely contemporary but also past and future churches and
forms of church which are not simply geographical, such as the
traditional domestic church of the family or the new one of
'Basic Christian Community'. The interaction of past and present in preparing for future is critical to the pilgrim model.
While communion seems to give priority to local and global in
contemporary terms (communion of communions), its historical
and eschatological dimensions emphasise the tension between
past, present and future. In discussion on governance the voices
of the past must be carefully listened to but so must the voices of
the present, as the pilgrim peoples face into the next phase of
their journey and seek to discern and express communion
among themselves at so many different levels.

Civil structures, church governance and the reign of God
In the historical discernment of communion and governance,
the believing community strove first of all to follow the practice
and teaching of Jesus as expressed in the apostolic witness of the
New Testament. Secondly, it sought to respond to the needs of
the people under the guidance of the Holy Spirit. Thirdly it interacted in critique and adaptation with contemporary 'secular'
civil insights, structures and practices. Fellowship with the excluded and new understanding of leadership (not lording like
the Gentiles or saying but not doing like the scribes and
Pharisees) exemplify the first strand. The emergence of diverse
ministries in the New Testament churches themselves and their
solidification into bishops, presbyters and deacons through the
second and into the third century, with the overlapping and
gradual emergence of the association of the Petrine primacy
with the see of Rome, provide examples of the second strand.

The third strand always in operation at least as critique became more obvious with the emergence of the churches from the catacombs into the basilicas, and the subsequent responsibility which church leaders had to assume for peace and order in the wider society. Monarch-like bishops and popes were the ambiguous fruits of these developments in ways which are still quite influential.

What needs to be stressed here is not the mistakes which were made, which tend to be exaggerated and some of which were in any case inevitable, but the necessity and appropriateness of the church learning and adapting, critically of course, from governing structures and practices of a particular time. As the scriptures and history indicate, the *kaine koinonia* (new community) initiated by Jesus did not have a clear and complete blueprint for the church to come. You cannot move directly, for example, from the gospels to the *Code of Canon Law* or even to *Lumen Gentium*. In following the Spirit the church did and could borrow from what it considered useful (sometimes uncritically perhaps) from the governing and organising structures of the wider society. It could justify this theologically if it cared to by the doctrines of creation and the reign of God. As it adopted Natural Law as a basis for personal and social morality, including the morality of civil governance, it could and did integrate elements of that kind of governance into its own life. The development of Canon Law itself is testimony to this. More interesting here may be the theological significance of the reign of God. This was the leading edge of Jesus' teaching and mission. The *koinonia* was to proclaim and promote the regin of God which had already been initiated and was yet to be completed. The church is at once the sign or sacrament as well as the proclaimer and promoter of the reign or presence of God in power creating, sustaining, healing and transforming the universe, God's creation. Given the scope of this mission it is clear that it cannot come from or within the church alone. The church is to discern and serve the coming of that kingdom or reign. Even on earth and in history the kingdom is coming in ways and areas outside the limits of the church. The healing dimensions of the reign inaugurated by Jesus, for example, cannot be confined to church even though the church played and can still play an honourable role with the medical profession in that particular healing service.

Where governance is concerned, some contemporary developments can reflect the emerging reign of God. Fresh insight into and respect for the dignity of the human being, with the accompanying recognition of certain inalienable human rights, including the right to participation in social governance, have yet to be realised properly and fully in our societies. Yet their development, however incomplete and even ambiguous, can be seen as *indicia regni Dei,* signs of the inbreaking reign of God. As such should they not play their due part in governance of the church? Is this not all the more true if the church is to be discerner and exemplar (sacrament) of God's reign as well as sacrament of the community of the whole human race (Vatican II)?

A further insight into the social and organisational dignity of the human being may be learned from the best management theories and practices where these are genuinely respectful and promoting of human dignity and freedom. As such they can reveal something, however limited, of the emerging kingdom of God and can be rightfully if critically integrated into the structures of the church. Participation and subsidiarity, already part of the church's moral vocabulary, should combine with good labour relations and efficient use of resources in church organisation also as it develops management skills and practices respectful of the human dignity of all its members and geared to its particular mission of promoting the reign of God.

The rhetoric of service and the harsh reality of serving
Managerial skills, for all their value, cannot replace the true Christian understanding and practice of governance as ministry or service. The persistent danger is that the rhetoric of service will replace the harsh reality of serving. It is still very difficult for lay people to recognise in the privileges and practices of priests, bishops and pope their proclaimed status as servants. It is also very difficult for these clergy themselves to escape anti-Christian delusions which they have inherited. Church leaders are not the only leaders with this kind of problem. Political ministers, presidents and bureaucrats are equally prone to delusions of power and grandeur at the expense of service. However, it was to leaders of the believing community that the warning about lording was issued. As sacrament of the whole to-be-redeemed human community, resort to lording power and privilege is a double betrayal of the church of Jesus Christ and of the human community. To compound the failure, the better civil

systems have developed corrective processes like constitutions and laws to which all are equally subject, accountability to their people at least through parliament, the media and the courts, the final verdict of regular elections. This is not to say that all is perfect or even healthy in our democratic civil systems but that they have values and practices which the believing community should consider and even endorse for the health of its own internal life and the effectiveness of its kingdom mission. In the search for immediate models of leadership, however, church leaders might concentrate on the least ones, the largely neglected and often ignored workers, the street-cleaners and domestics, the shop assistants and the waitresses, the single working mothers and the struggling unemployed in search of work and acceptance in society, for whom lording and ladying are not really options.

The recurring risk of God
'In the beginning God and in the end God' describes the reach of Christian community, life and faith. It sets the limits for the discussion and reform of church govemance also. The difficulty is deciphering where these limits fare, where the Spirit of God is leading us in this and in many other matters. Recognition of God as incomprehensible mystery and as Lord of history requires endless humility in seeking to decipher divine ways. The lessons of history suggest a God of surprises. The greatest surprise of all was God's initiative in Jesus. At the heart of that surprise lies Calvary. The risks God undertook in creation and redemption are finally revealed here. The risks demanded of the believing community in response are deep and searching. Yet it will not be tested beyond that for which, in the strength of the Spirit of God, it is able. The recurring risk of God is both challenge and grace. In that spirit of hope, renewal of church governance is called for and enabled.

CHAPTER FOUR

Prophecy or Politics?
The Role of the Churches in Society

Some of Stanley Hauerwas's most provocative and illuminating work has focused on the public role of the church, on the *Ekklesia* and *Polis*, on *Ekklesia* as *Polis* to adapt a title of one of his recent books. Much of my own work has dealt with similar problems, reaching back to my doctoral dissertation of 1960 on *Church and State in the Constitution of Ireland*. With different ecclesiological backgrounds (Methodist and Catholic), different political contexts and challenges (primarily the United States and Ireland) and different theological *personae,* we have followed quite different paths and arrived at quite different if provisional perspectives. Yet I continue to read Stanley with considerable sympathy and profit, while finding that I have to struggle with my own problems in my own context. This essay is not then a critical evaluation of the Hauerwas contribution to the American and wider debate on church and society, or however he might phrase it. I do not feel equal to that. It is something much less ambitious, an effort to discover for myself first of all where I stand on the role of the churches in society (my phrase) after forty years of struggle in practice as well as in theory. It is the best way I know to pay tribute to more than twenty years of personal friendship and theological enrichment.

Catholic theology and social engagement
Without attempting an analysis of 'One Hundred Years of Catholic Social Teaching', as it is sometimes called, still less any serious reflection on the much longer and more tangled tradition of the relation between Christian/Catholic faith and social justice, the concern here is with certain developments in this relationship which have occurred in the working life of this theologian. The justification for this is two-fold: the significance of the shifts that have occurred in theory (theology) and practice (engagement) in the relationship during this period and the theologian's own experience of them in theory and practice.

The 1950s were not particularly exciting years for the student of Catholic theology in Ireland. The post-war European ferment-ation already bubbling did not really affect undergraduate theo-logy. This was heavily neo-scholastic but not exclusively so. It did in hindsight correspond rather closely to the non-historical orthodoxy attributed in the 1960s to the Roman schools of theol-ogy by Michael Novak. More relevantly here academic theology was sharply separated from practice, understood in a rather nar-row pastoral and sacramental sense. Even moral theology, pro-fessedly the most practical of theological disciplines, was largely concerned with categorising personal sins for confessional pur-poses. Personal moral development was not discussed and social justice issues were for an entirely separate and by definition non-theological course in Catholic Social Teaching. In some sig-nificant sense theology had been privatised in the language used by John Baptist Metz and other 'political theologians' later in the 1960s.

Ireland and Maynooth, however, were not so easily pigeon-holed. The Catholic Church in Ireland, lay and clerical, had a long history of social involvement. The struggles for democratic participation led by Daniel O'Connell, a layman, depended for its effective organisation on church leaders, especially priests in their parishes. This combination of a Catholic laity and clergy in promotion of democracy in the early nineteenth century in Ireland was greatly admired by people like Lacordaire and others in Europe. Subsequent struggles throughout the nineteenth century for educational, social and economic development con-tinued, in varying forms and degrees, this alliance between politicians and clergy as community leaders. Although the bulk of the clergy and perhaps all the bishops rejected the armed struggle as a legitimate means of political social change, it had its clerical and theological defenders, at least post-factum. While this was dominantly a nationalist-Catholic alliance, clergy and laity from the Reformed churches in Ireland, Presbyterian, Church of Ireland and Methodist, played key roles in the nation-alist political, cultural and economic enterprise. This bore fruit in the relatively tolerant laws and constitution of the new state, despite some serious counter-examples in law and social prac-tice.

The partition of Ireland, with six north-eastern counties re-taining political union with Great Britain, had political roots and consequences which influenced considerably the relationships of all the churches with the two political entities, the Republic of Ireland and Northern Ireland, as they are now usually called. Within Northern Ireland, Protestants were overwhelmingly unionist, Catholics were overwhelmingly nationalist. The coincidence of political and religious affiliation on both sides of the border made for a very troubled relationship which erupted in the violent troubles of the last thirty years in Northern Ireland. In the south, or the Republic, the tension and trouble was much less, partly because of the tiny proportion of Protestants and partly because after independence 'bread-and-butter politics' gradually replaced republican and unionist ideals or ideologies. In the Republic points of tension remained, to be sometimes inflamed by events, north and south, such as Bloody Sunday in Derry (Northern Ireland) 1972 or the Fethard-on-Sea boycott of Protestants in 1957 (the Republic).

These scraps of Irish history may help in understanding why and how some Irish students of theology, even in the 1950s, were prompted to stray beyond the confines of 'pure' theology and engage theologically with the social and political situation. In that spirit this theologian undertook a doctoral dissertation on early Anglican theology in the Theology Faculty at Maynooth and followed it up with one on church-state relations in the Canon Law Faculty at the University of Munich. With the acumen with which some church and even university administrators sometimes operate, the end-result of all this was a teaching post in moral theology in the Faculty at Maynooth. Earlier engagements were not neglected as a series of articles on church-state relations in the sixties and two books on *Roman Catholics and Unity* (London, 1962) and *Religious Liberty* (London, 1967) attest.

The intersection of the Catholic theological tradition and the Irish political tradition influenced how Irish theologians related Catholic theology and social engagement. It influenced but it did not initiate or determine it. Indeed divisions in Catholicism on this matter were already evident in public debate in Ireland. Since the introduction of the new Constitution of Ireland in 1937, which failed to establish the Catholic Church as the official state church, or as the true church in the phrase of some advocates, there had been a campaign to have this amended and the Catholic Church duly recognised. In theological lecture hall and journal this became a disputed point also. For the proponents of 'establishment', the manuals of Public Ecclesiastic Law of Cardinal Alfredo Ottaviani, Head of the Holy Office, as it was then called, and sundry nineteenth-century predecessors were source and authority. For their opponents, the new situation of democracy, the experience of churches free of involvement with the state and the reflections of Jacques Maritain, John Courtney Murray and others suggested new relationships between church and state, new ways of being church in the world, fresh insights into theology's social engagement.

In a semi-autobiographical essay, the chronology of personal concern and involvement may provide the easier and indeed clearer line of argument. The case for recognition of the Catholic Church as the one true church, as advanced by Ottaviani and others in Europe and by J. C. Fenton *et al* in the USA, had surfaced in Ireland but was rejected by Eamon de Valera for the Constitution adopted by the people of Ireland in 1937. The debate rumbled on into the fifties. The very terms involved for church and state were looking increasingly unreal, each a perfect society in its own sphere with its own end and the means to that end. The one supernatural and the other natural, each had independent responsibility in its own sphere. As they served the same people they ought to co-operate; in case of conflict the supernatural as superior ought to prevail. There were softer expressions of the theory but the essentials remained the same. In practice all kinds of accommodation were made, *faute de mieux*.

Early attempts to refute this position were partly inspired by the conviction that it was inapplicable in the Republic of Ireland despite its ninety-five percent Catholic majority, and partly by what appeared to be double standards in claiming religious freedom for Catholics when in a minority and refusing it, or at least restricting it, for others when Catholics were in a majority and the Catholic Church became 'established'. The re-reading of the work of Leo XIII by John Courtney Murray, tortuous as it appeared at times, enabled a more robust magisterial defence of the separation of church and state and of religious freedom than seemed possible when the debate was first aired in the halls of Maynooth by Jeremiah Newman, later Bishop of Limerick. Much gratitude is due to Newman for introducing students so quickly to that debate and for his continuing friendship despite deep and lasting disagreement about the issues.

Murray was naturally influenced by the American experience in which the Catholic Church thrived on freedom rather than privilege. The state he argued was incompetent in religious matters and so could not determine which was the one true church in order to establish it. The church best exercised its influence through its members who were citizens and legislators not through formal recognition or legally binding agreements like concordats. Murray endorsed religious freedom as a citizen's right in relation to the state to profess and practise any religion or none within the limits of public order. This is the heart of Vatican II's document on religious liberty of which Murray was the chief architect. For all his regard for certain aspects of the liberal tradition and for human rights in general, Murray was no defender of a simple liberal individualism or of rights language as a comprehensive political language. He recognised the state's obligation to the good of the whole community as expressed in public order for example. The moral values which the state should protect would, in his thinking, correspond to the central values of the natural law tradition. This is a feature exemplified in much recent papal and episcopal teaching.

Religious freedom, defined and defended along the Murray lines, had further implications for understanding church, state and their relationships. Some of these were already anticipated in the work of Jacques Maritain on Christian faith, democracy and human rights. Maritain was even less of an ideological liberal than Murray but he had a genuine sense of the value of democracy and of personal human rights, which owed much to his reading of St Thomas and the natural law tradition. In particular he alerted one to the limits of the state, not by the church primarily but by its role as the servant of society or wider community. The distinction between society and state, and the priority of society as the people in its overlapping structures and relationships, was widely accepted in western democratic theory, if not always in practice. Its relation to the original Christian claim for freedom to worship its own God while asserting its loyalty to empire and emperor was not always given due credit by defenders of democracy, Christian or non-Christian. In the further development of Christian understanding of the role of the churches in society, the distinction between society and state beyond any Constantinian accommodation was bound to be crucial. (The Irish version of this may have escaped Stanley

Hauerwas in his romantic recall of Confirmation day in Sneem, County Kerry).

The distinction between society and state, with its implications for the defence of human rights, personal and social, was, whatever its remote origins, now a political and secular reality. A church shaped by a Constantinian polity did not necessarily fit. Understanding of the church was also changing. For Catholic theology, Vatican II was crucial to this. And for the purposes of this essay, perhaps the more crucial was the *Pastoral Constitution on the Church in the Modern World* rather than the *Dogmatic Constitution on the Church*. The recovery of the image of the church as the pilgrim people of God cleared the way for a possible alternative and prophetic vision of its role in society in preference to the persisting Constantinian model, however diluted.

The diluted Constantinian model could be discerned in both the theology and practice of church-state relations after as well as before Vatican II. It still survives in more attenuated forms where civil governments and church leaders have formal or informal arrangements on issues like education, social welfare, health, on particular offices like chaplaincies to parliament or to the army, or laws restricting specific 'immoral' activities as crimes. At least some of this may still be justifiable but all of it will need re-examining in the context of church, state and society undergoing constant change.

The *Declaration on Religious Freedom* defended against any state coercion the right of the individual citizen and community to freedom of faith and its public expression, within the limits of public order and morality. This both resolved a problem and displaced it from the religious to the moral arena. Christianity's inextricable link with morality and the understanding by the Catholic Church and by Catholic theology of natural law as applicable to all human beings, combined with that church' s claim to be the authoritative interpreter of natural law, ensured many sharp disputes in the Western world between state legislators and church leaders, in particular on issues such as divorce, contraception, abortion and homosexuality. Justice and peace issues such as poverty, racism, militarism and discrimination against women were sometimes the sources of church criticism of state authorities but seldom with the same intensity and persistence, or above all with the same vocal support of the church membership. In the Irish debates which came later than those in the rest

of the Western world, neither side learned much from what had
happened elsewhere in Europe and North America.

Praxis and theory: Theology's uncertainty principle
The recent sharp theological debate on the relation between
praxis and theory, prompted in particular by the development
of Liberation Theology in Latin America and undoubtedly influenced by earlier Marxist ideas, had its own if latterly latent
Christian origins and tradition. Faith in Jesus Christ meant discipleship, a way of life, a praxis. Understanding at this basic level
of acceptance of his claims simultaneously involved acceptance
of his lifestyle. Theory or intellectual recognition was inextrica-
bly linked with praxis. Even within the gospels themselves and
among his closest and most avid disciples, there were failures in
faith and following. The ambition of the Sons of Thunder to sit at
his right hand and left when he should come into his kingdom,
or Peter's denial at the trial so soon after his boast of loyalty,
might be interpreted as first of all failure in either faith or following or more plausibly in both. However, the distinction between
moral failure and loss of faith was an early part of the way of
discipleship and provided a basis for what might be called a distinction between theory and praxis. In contemporary terms, Irish
playwright Brendan Behan's remark that he had 'the honour to
be a bad Catholic' is in that tradition of distinguishing faith from
morality. To deny the distinction leads to a puritanical and un-
forgiving church far from the koinonia of love envisaged in the
New Testament. To separate faith and morality leads to corrupt
Christians and a corrupt church which have surfaced too frequently in history and is no less unfaithful to the promise of the
New Testament. Like faith and morality, Christian theory and
praxis belong together although it is never easy to determine at a
particular juncture which if either has priority in what might be
described as a communion of sinners struggling to be a communion of saints.

Although faith/morality are close correlates of theory/praxis
in Christian discourse, the theory/praxis distinction in current
usage has tended to operate at a more self-consciously intellectual or at least analytic level. At this level they remain also inex-
tricably bound together, while the question of which gets prior
attention also depends on the particular situation. Indeed to
focus on the one affects understanding of the other in a way that

may be said to be crudely analagous to how concentration on the speed of a subatomic particle interferes with the exact observation of its location. To speak of theology's uncertainty principle on such an analogy is indeed crude. It has the merit of drawing attention not only to the mutual influence of Christian theology (usually presented as theory) and Christian living (sometimes described as praxis). It also exposes the difficulties of providing both a settled theology and practice as dimensions of one or other change.

For the first Christian communities, the acceptance of Gentile converts free of regular Jewish obligations, or the debates about eating meat sacrificed to idols, offered classic instances of the interaction of theology and Christian practice. What began as debated practice ended in changing the theological understanding. And so it was that the early Christians made their way uncertainly in the world of the frequently hostile Roman Empire. The development of the second plank of salvation, as Tertullian called it, with the practice of the sacrament of Penance not only confirmed the distinction and relationship between faith and morality but promoted a deeper understanding of the teaching and practice of Jesus' saving and forgiving mission. Later developments from public to private penance illustrated further the changing relationship between theory and praxis which continued to characterise the life of the Christian community. Not all of these interactions were faith-enhancing or life-giving to the community, as the many corrupt historical practices and attempts at their theological justification demonstrated. The Reformation divisions over indulgences involved a notable example of how corrupt practice can corrupt faith. Even four hundred years later there has not been an entirely satisfactory solution to the problems posed by the practice and theory of indulgences then. However, the decline of the practice among the Catholic faithful has prompted neglect by theologians of the traditional forms of explanation and near silence among preachers and bishops of this once trumpeted way of development in the Christian life. Practice and theology move in parallel here as indeed they do in the almost dormant state which the Catholic Church is experiencing in regard to the practice and theology of the sacrament of private penance. These are the developments primarily of particular times and places, the late twentieth century in the Western world. Their future here is as unpredictable

as the retention of some of the older understanding and practice
is in other parts of the Catholic world. What is significant is the
mutual influence for change of Catholic theology and practice in
diverse social and cultural situations. That is the certainty and
the uncertainty which church and theology must always expect
to experience on their pilgrim ways.

Although they were influenced by their social and cultural
situations and had their own social and cultural impact in turn,
the examples examined of the interaction between theory and
praxis in Christian tradition were primarily internal to the
church and only indirectly related to the political arena. This
would need much further explication and qualification as one
recalls the unconditional acceptance of non-Jews and its impact
on the Roman Empire and the public continuation of Judaism.
Inherently religious as the development of the sacrament of
penance might appear, the order of public penitents and the
summons of the Emperor to Canossa had profound political implications. It was the formal entry of the church into the public
life of the Roman Empire in the fourth century which made the
social engagement and praxis of the church so significant for its
self-understanding, its theory or theology. Indeed as indicated
earlier, the remnants of this development were evident in the
theory and praxis of church-state relations well into the twentieth
century and have not yet entirely disappeared.

The most striking instance of change in church theory and
practice, prompted by the change in church-empire relations,
was the development of the just war theory and practice. During
its first centuries, the church maintained a basically pacifist
stance. This was in fidelity to the teaching and practice of Jesus,
but also influenced by the Roman army's profession of Caesar as
divine. With Christians taking on responsibilities for administration of the empire and the emperor himself becoming
Christian, many Christian leaders began to reconsider this purely
pacifist role which had begun to be eroded in practice on the
margins of the empire even earlier. Ambrose and Augustine
were notable early leaders in justifying the use of arms at least in
defence. The detailed development of just war theory through
the centuries and by such outstanding thinkers as Aquinas were
at least as much attempts to restrain the practice as to justify it.
The practice it must be said outran the theory and the theological criteria were readily distorted or ignored. Right into our own

decade theology has limped behind practice in the initiation and conduct of war by political leaders who would consider themselves Christian. It has been on rare occasions that church leaders have had the courage to criticise the war-making of their own state, despite the formal and informal separations of church and state.

The search for a new paradigm
In personal terms the inadequacies of just war theory in face of the actuality of war, and the repeated tendencies of churches to justify their own side, raised serious questions not only about any form, however diluted, of traditional church-state relations but about the terms in which the whole debate and actual relationships were cast. These questions were not easily formulated or answered. Some critical experiences at home in Ireland and abroad, particularly in Africa, suggested serious adaptation of older models and then rapidly exposed the weakness of the new.

The Irish experience
Over the last thirty years and more Irish experiences, north and south, however different they might be, contributed to the rethinking of the relations between church and state in ways which may be relevant well beyond the island. Partition introduced by the British in 1921 resulted in what many people perceived as two confessional if not sectarian states, Northern Ireland with its own parliament and government within the United Kingdom and subject to the British monarch in parliament at Westminster, and what was eventually declared in 1949 to be the Republic of Ireland, a fully autonomous state with its parliament in Dublin. The religious influence on the legislation and administration of the two states may still be sharply debated but undoubtedly the near Protestant homogeneity of the unionist majority in the north and the near Catholic homogeneity of the nationalist majority in the south ensured very close relations between the respective church and state leaders which inevitably created difficulties for and between the churches and the states.

In the south, or more properly the Republic, the difficulties focused on law and morality issues, particularly issues of sexual morality. Much of the Republic's law in this area had been inherited from the British regime, although the Constitution of 1937 had introduced a new element by banning the passing of a law permitting divorce. Debates on these issues began in the 1960s and dragged on until the passing of the referendum allowing divorce in 1995. Catholic Church leaders opposed these changes although not on religious grounds but on those of natural law or of damage to society or the public good. Protestant Church leaders for the most part endorsed the changes, again not on religious grounds but on those of individual human rights or of the lesser damage to the public good. The arguments advanced on both sides had their merits but there was clearly a certain amount of too easy coincidence between the moral positions of the different churches and their attitudes to legal change. Of course church leaders were not the only ones in these debates who might be accused of adopting self-interested positions. Politicians and citizens, conservative and liberal, were often pursuing interests other than human rights or the public good. This kind of ambiguity is inevitable in such debates. To call attention to it is not to impugn the good faith of either side but to encourage a more tolerant attitude to difference and to discourage the kind of self-righteousness which is sadly seldom avoided in such situations. It was not avoided in Ireland.

The political nature and the frequently hostile and self-righteous tone of the debates exposed the Catholic Church in particular to the accusation of being simply another self-interested and power-seeking social force. However justified such accusation might be, and it could be and was strongly contested, the image of the church as herald of the good news of salvation and healer of a broken humanity was badly damaged. The clerical sexual scandals including paedophilia which became a feature of the 1990s added the accusation of hypocrisy to a church leadership which had taken such a hard line on sexual morality and legal change in this area. The humbler church which many clerics and church members called for would have to find a new and radically changed role in society to replace the once cosy relationship with the state.

The developments through Maritain and Murray, documents such as John XXIII's *Pacem in Terris* and those on Religious Freedom and on the Church in the Modern World had, without offering a blueprint, opened up again the distinction between society and state and at least pointed to the proper role of the church as operating freely in society rather than seeking power-agreements with the state. Indeed it became increasingly clearer

that the defence of personal freedoms and the defining and seeking of the public good depended on seeing the state and its institutions as the servants rather than the masters of society, where
society was understood as the totality of the people within the
territory in which the state was recognised, with all that people's
complexity of culture, religion and voluntary organisation. In
such a society the church could claim freedom to preach, to worship and to organise on the same basis as other religious traditions without claiming in state law any privileges for itself. Its
further roles in society would depend on the traditions of that
society where a symbolic role might be appropriate on certain
national occasions or where it might offer educational and social
services endorsed by the people. The state might and perhaps
should be neutral religiously but the society would reflect the
plurality and social value of the religions of its peoples. As servant of society the state would respect its people's traditions as
long as they did not violate the human rights of others and the
good of the society as a whole.

Of course in practice in Ireland as in so many other countries
such an approach was bound to leave many loose ends, as for
example the precise definition and reach of a particular human
right and how it differed, if it did, from a civil right. Some people
argued in the Irish debate that divorce was a civil right due
under the law here and now, but not necessarily a human right
deriving from the nature of the human person and demanded
under any civil law, anytime, anywhere. More complex issues
arise with claims of a person's right over one's own body and
the translation of this into a right to abortion, an issue still unset-
tled in Irish law. Similar difficulties emerge in any discussion of
the public good, although the new batch of Irish controversies
over corruption in politics and business and over the provisions
for the indigenous deprived and the newly arriving immigrants
and asylum-seekers, may allow for more objective and fruitful
debates than former heated sexual ones did.

Theologically the theologians and documents cited did not
entirely escape the shadow of Constantinianism. This was more
an achievement of the 1970s and later. In particular the humbler
role of the church, which it was being forced to recognise in
Ireland, could appear to be no more than a political tactic without a fuller theological understanding of what that humble role
of servant might mean. For this a return to the theology of the

reign of God as originally preached by Jesus was necessary. This
did occur to some extent in Ireland but more in the context of the
'Troubles' in Northern Ireland and the inter-church problems
which they involved.

Protestant and Catholic divisions in Northern Ireland were
closely intertwined with the political divisions so that the Civil
Rights marches by nationalists/Catholics began in the late sixties in protest at the discrimination against them by the union-
ist/Protestant government.

Ordinary Catholic Church members composed the bulk of
the protesters with at least tacit support from many of the clergy.
Opponents of the protests, both police and citizens, were dominantly unionist/Protestant with very loud support from some of
the more extreme Protestant clergy. As protest and counter-
protest eventually degenerated into violent campaigns by both
sides, which have only recently ended, church members and
leaders faced more difficult decisions. The majority, lay and clerical, disowned and increasingly denounced the violence but
their credibility to the other side was damaged by their apparent
support for the objectives of the men of violence, United
Kingdom v United Ireland. Many individual clerics and lay
Christians sought to promote inter-church relations as a way of
distancing the churches from the disputes and so of removing
one source of the tension. This had some impact but very little
hard thinking or self-sacrificial practice followed. The churches
remained for the most part captive to their own peoples, chaplains to their own tribes in a form of post-Constantinianism.

An attempt was made by some Catholic commentators to
apply Latin American liberation theology to the Northern
Ireland situation. Religious division and its presence among the
poorest and most oppressed made it very difficult if not impossible to claim Jesus as liberator for just one side. The actual violence on both sides obscured such Christian claims also.
Recourse was had to the theory of just war by republican supporters, even in response to Pope John Paul II's powerful plea
for a peaceful search for justice. As the relations between the
churches continued to exacerbate the differences, some theological relativising of the churches seemed imperative. The role of
the churches in society had to be properly subordinated to the
reign of God preached and inaugurated by Jesus. In the service
of that reign, they were called to work together in society with-

out necessarily betraying their own identities. The churches would not then relate primarily to state or tribe but to the reign of God as it sought to emerge through peace and justice in society. Such theology and its implementation did not develop to any great degree in Ireland, north or south.

The African experience
In the late sixties the Catholic Church in South Africa established a series of Winter Schools in theology to help bring the theology of Vatican II to its clergy and people. In 1970 Bishop Christopher Butler and myself were invited to offer together a week's course in six centres. As the moral theologian on the team, I was faced with responding to the moral dilemmas confronting the South African church. As this was my first visit and my first exposure to the apartheid system, I saw it as South Africa's primary moral challenge. So did many of the participants in the various schools we attended. Yet its public discussion was muted compared with that of a number of sexual and marital issues like divorce and particularly contraception. Two years after *Humanae Vitae,* bishops, clergy and laity were still animatedly discussing how far contraceptives might be used by married couples in particular situations. In trying to help the South African church with these two moral difficulties, some clarity emerged about the different attitudes involved and the divided approaches adopted. For the majority of the bishops and clergy, opposition to apartheid was real but muted as the more prudent and effective way of protecting the African peoples against its worst excesses and promoting gradual change in its theory and practice. There were of course significant exceptions to this approach at the different levels of the church who advocated a more radical and vocal opposition to a great injustice. In regard to *Humanae Vitae,* the majority (smaller perhaps) adopted the radical and uncompromising line of no exceptions while a large minority favoured a softer line of approval of contraceptives in exceptional circumstances. Generally speaking whose who favoured the more muted approach on apartheid were the uncompromising on contraception, while the radical opponents of apartheid tended to be more lenient on contraception. The divisions within the South African church on such issues were not peculiar to it. In reflecting subsequently on the different reactions, the more radical whether in opposition to

apartheid or contraception, had the ring of the prophetic tradition of Israel and the church, while the more lenient and accommodating to immediate circumstances belonged rather to the Wisdom tradition of Israel and church. All this would require much more analysis and qualification to which further African experiences would contribute.

In the 1970s there came an invitation from the Catholic Institute of International Relations in London to work with the Justice and Peace Commission of the church in Rhodesia, as it then was, on moral aspects of the war between the Smith Regime which had seized power in 1965 and the guerrillas fighting for an independent Zimbabwe, as it was to be called. Over a seven-year period, involving a number of extensive visits to the country, I prepared a report on the war and eventually a book on the relations between church and society.

In studying the moral legitimacy of the origins and conduct of the war, I encountered very deep divisions among church leaders and members. My own conclusion, that on the application of just war criteria the war of independence could be termed a just war, was qualified by my reservation about war being an appropriate way for Christians to deal with these matters. It was perhaps another example of the distinction between the wisdom tradition accepting war as justified in extreme circumstances and the prophetic call to seek alternatives.

The Rhodesian situation, with neither of the warring groups able to claim international recognition as state, emphasised more deeply the distinction between state and society. The church however had its difficult role to fulfil in preaching and promoting justice and peace, the message and substance of the reign of God in society. In this context the four distinct elements in theological social analysis and engagement were more clearly discernible, church as community of disciples in service of the coming reign of God within a society which would be served by a newly legitimised state. When the new state of Zimbabwe emerged the church still had the task of preaching and promoting the reign of God. The behaviour of the new state did not always make that easy but it did make it more necessary. How far the Zimbabwean church fulfilled its task in a spirit of wisdom, as the new state sought to establish itself, and in a spirit of prophecy if fresh injustices appeared, I am not now in a position to judge.

The church's call to preach and promote the reign of God as preached by Jesus was being developed more radically during this time first of all by Latin American theologians in what came to be known as liberation theology. Their emphasis on doing theology from the perspective of the poor and oppressed, and their insistence on the primacy of praxis, engagement in the struggle for liberation as the starting point for theology, began to influence theology throughout the church. In other third world countries in Africa and Asia, as well as among oppressed communities in the first world such as women and African and Hispanic-Americans, liberation theology in different forms offered the profoundest challenge so far to the lingering elements of Constantinian relations between church and state. In the new world of liberal capitalism and its version of globalisation, liberation theology became the instrument of the poor in prodding the church into opposing the economic oppressions of the powerful nations and corporations. The Catholic Church always had a global role in service of the universal reign of God. That would have to assume a particular prophetic form in the vision of liberation theologians and in the light of the dominantly economic shape which globalisation is assuming. My latest round of African experiences over the last decade may shed some further light on that prophetic role.

As a member of the Caritas Internationalis Task Force on HIV and AIDS, I have been working as theological and ethical advisor with educational programmes for AIDS carers and community leaders, including church leaders in third world countries mainly in Africa, throughout the 1990s. The theological-ethical problems are multiple and complex. The two discussed here relate to issues discussed earlier and help illustrate once more the role of the church in an entirely new context, the AIDS-ravaged situation of Sub-Saharan Africa.

The concern and commitment of the church in these African countries in the fight against HIV and AIDS can be impressive in its education, prevention and caring programmes, particularly given its puny resources and the other massive health, education and poverty problems these countries face. However, one typical ethical difficulty recurs, that is the use of condoms as a means of prevention and the co-operation with public health programmes which promote their use. Many bishops and other Catholics oppose their use as a violation of the teaching of

Humanae Vitae, as likely to increase promiscuity and so the spread of HIV and AIDS, and as unreliable in any event. Faithfulness in marriage and abstinence outside it is the only secure moral way. This last prophetic message needs to be preached and repeated but it will not halt or much diminish the spread of the infection in the cultural and social circumstances of many current African situations. Meantime the prudent promotion and use of condoms in Uganda, for example, has helped at least to stabilise the spread. From a theological point of view, the use of condoms in AIDS-prevention programmes is far removed from the spirit and the letter of *Humanae Vitae*. The encyclical deals with the prevention of life-giving, the AIDS-prevention programmes with the prevention of death-dealing. In the older wisdom theology of choosing the lesser evil where evil is going to occur in any event, condoms should be advised to reduce the risk of infection. They are not entirely safe but they are safer if of good quality and properly used. This is the wisdom message which the church also needs to articulate.

The condoms issue is a significant but still minor one in the overall ethical and theological discussion of HIV and AIDS in Africa. On a quite different plane, it is becoming gradually clearer that the greatest obstacle to fighting and overcoming the pandemic in these countries is poverty. HIV and AIDS are becoming increasingly a feature of the poor and not only in the third world as the figures for African and Hispanic-Americans confirm. The areas and groups listed in recent UN Reports on Human Development as most deprived under a wide range of headings coincide to a great extent with the areas and groups listed by UNAIDS and other reports as most affected by the virus. Without major and sustainable development, the poor countries will fail to serve or even preserve their people in face of this and other disasters, human and natural.

CHAPTER FIVE

Invite and Encourage

The disappointment which many Catholics and members of other Christian churches experienced on the publication by the Episcopal Conferences of Ireland, England and Wales and Scotland of *One Bread, One Body: A teaching document on the Eucharist*, was given widespread public expression at the time, September-October 1998. The reasons offered for the disappointment were multiple and complex. It was a strong document, not just in its (widely unwelcome) negative regulations on eucharistic sharing, but in its (widely welcomed) positive teaching on the eucharist itself. This conflict of strengths was compounded by a conflict of source and timing. For the first major inter-island Catholic Church document to emerge in the aftermath of the Good Friday Peace Agreement should have been a reinforcement of the process had it not been so restrictive of practices already developing and so inevitably offensive to 'sister' churches. In a situation where political settlement within Northern Ireland and between Ireland and Britain was and is still so delicately poised, and where the churches have always been part of the problem, more generous practical directives, or a patient and silent waiting upon the working of the Spirit among all God's people, would have been more gospel-like. The belief that consultation was as usual unnecessarily limited and that canonical regulation finally took precedence over theological agreement or pastoral awareness seem borne out by the structure and content of the document itself.

Conversion and convergence
The extraordinary reversal in inter-church relations which Vatican II's *Decree on Ecumenism* represented for the Catholic Church has proved astonishingly fruitful. From a situation in which a Catholic might not enter a Protestant church even for the funeral of a friend, or say the Lord's Prayer with fellow

Christians, that church moved rapidly to joint prayer services, to open and serious dialogue on doctrinal differences and to regular co-operation on social issues. Christ's prayer that they might be one so that the world might believe seemed a short time away. Conversion to one another, *metanoia,* a radical change of mind and heart, between Christians and 'ecclesial' communities or churches, had come about suddenly and unexpectedly as a gift of the Spirit working through a range of ecumenical pioneers, without and within the Catholic Church. The gift of conversion enabled the continuing work of convergence in prayer, worship and doctrine, in pastoral and social engagement. What began as co-operation and convergence frequently issued in mutual understanding, agreed statements and spiritual bonds which were, at least for the immediate parties involved, new stages of conversion. However, the larger unity at official levels in the churches did not move so rapidly. The continuing requests for clarification, the clouding by qualifications and the persistence of negative regulations left many Catholics with the growing feeling that that first conversion of Vatican II had run out of energy and no fresh conversion was at hand. This appeared to be most sharply illustrated in refusal of shared eucharist despite the range and depth of carefully negotiated and agreed statements by commissions appointed officially by the churches themselves. The absence of any sense of such conversion to other churches in *One Bread, One Body,* despite its informed theological discussion, may be the key to its failure to convince so many.

Conversion: Christian and human
Conversion is a very dangerous word to use in discussing ecumenism. For many Christian believers ecumenism itself has superseded conversion. To speak of, and still more to promote, conversion sounds anti-ecumenical. This is because hitherto conversion in inter-church relations meant changing church allegiance. In the pre-Vatican II era Catholics in these islands cherished a certain triumphalist feeling about converts from other churches, particularly if they were clergy, intellectuals, artists or writers – preferably all three or four. Ronald Knox was a key example. Such conversious still go on, and so they should, although they are not simply in one direction. They are to be honoured for what they are: painful and honest searches for the

fuller Christian truth. The receiving church should, of course, be welcoming and caring but without triumphalism, always an unChristian attitude.

In biblical and particularly New Testament terms, conversion has a more profound and extensive meaning. First of all it means a turning to God, Creator and Redeemer, the unknowable mystery who is origin and fulfilment of all. The eucharist is basically the sacrament of such conversion for all of humanity and indeed of creation. It is the sign of God's enabling gift reconciling the world with himself, a sign in continuity with and transformation of both the covenant of creation and the Mosaic covenant with Israel. One of the richer insights of contemporary theology of the eucharist, including several agreed statements and *One Bread, One Body,* is renewed emphasis on the links between the creation, Judaic and Christian covenants. The conversion dimension of the eucharist involves a reconciliation with the God of all peoples and of all creation. This universal dimension of eucharist may be easily overlooked in an excessively religious and exclusivist model. Mass on the world and of the world is not just a Teilhardian poetic fantasy.

For Christians, conversion to God takes place in and through conversion to Jesus Christ, through whom and in whom the world was both created and redeemed. His one unique sacrifice, remembered and re-enacted in the eucharist, reconciles and reunites God with the world. In celebrating the eucharist Christians are drawn into this continuing, mediating and transforming action of God in Christ. Doing this in remembrance of him is the central action of thc Christian community whereby they are identified and renewed as daughters and sons of the Father, sisters and brothers of Christ, temples of the Holy Spirit. Sharing the eucharist is the climax of their personal and community conversion to Jesus Christ and of the witness to the world of their conversion to one another.

Conversion to one another, which also translates as reconciliation with one another, is a continuing dynamic process of which the eucharist is the central Christian expression. For the baptised believers in Jesus Christ and in his saving, reconciling presence in the eucharist, sharing the eucharist is the crucial manifestation and means of that reconciliation. The thrust of this proposal is that members of other churches, with a basic belief in the eucharist as instituted by Jesus Christ, should be invited and

encouraged to participate in the Catholic eucharist as a manifestation and means of developing reconciliation between Christians
and of witnessing to the world. In similar fashion, Catholics
should be invited and encouraged to join in the eucharistic celebration of other churches and for the same reasons. Only with
such conversion process of eucharistic sharing may the hoped-
for millennial breakthrough in inter-church relations emerge
and new patterns in convergence, co-operation and community
develop. The theological basis for all this is already established
in the agreed statements, tested in many pastoral situations and
acknowledged in the exceptions in the 1993 Vatican *Directives*
for Ecumenism.

Body of Christ

Interpreting the ecumenical movement as a progressive conversion of the different churches and their members to one another
in Christ under the guidance of the Spirit is at once clarified and
obscured by their common membership through faith and baptism in the Body of Christ. It is clarified in that all Christians
need continuing conversion in and to Christ. It is obscured in
that their already shared membership of Christ seems to render
unnecessary, or at least less comprehensive, the kind of radical
conversion which the ecumenical movement demanded originally and which still seems to be needed afresh. In fact shared
membership in the Body of Christ is the basis of existing unity
and the source of hope and challenge for future, fuller unity. It is
difficult with this basis and this hope to refrain from inviting
Christians to share the sacramental Body of Christ, to eat what
they are, in Augustine's words.

Perhaps not enough has been made of our shared baptism.
Of course over the millennia, baptism celebrated by those separated from a particular church has generally been accepted as
valid by that church, that is as truly incorporating a person into
the Body of Christ. At first this was very practical in its consequences: such a baptised person was not, could not be rebap-
tised. In the aftermath of the Reformation divisions, the mutual
acceptance of baptism tended to disappear with conditional rebaptism often invoked. One of the many positive results of the
ecumenical movement has been the full restoration of mutual
acceptance of baptism without any of the offence and confusion
of conditional rebaptism. This welcome development demands

fuller practical, theological and liturgical expression. The call to further and deeper co-operation by all the baptised, in care of the world, human and physical, is a commonplace of ecumenical rhetoric. It needs more concrete realisation in some of the more painful areas of war and peace, of population growth and environmental destruction. That too has its sacramental and eucharistic implications in the continuity between creation and redemption of humanity and the cosmos.

The relevant theological insights have already been outlined. These insights require social and earthly expression of the kind just indicated. They also require ecclesial and liturgical expression of a kind too long neglected by the churches. In societies with a Christian component in their political and social divisions, like Northern Ireland and Bosnia, inter-church celebration of baptism could release vision and energy beyond the tunnel visions and destructive energies characteristic of so many close combinations of politics and religion. Apart from such divisive situations, the more secular worlds of the West and North and the often deeply religious worlds of the East and South could only be enriched by the joint celebration of the sacrament of integration into Christ's Body. Only then would the mutual acceptance of one another's baptism be given its proper (in the light of incarnation) visible, sacramental expression. The usual difficulties raised in regard to shared eucharist, such as precisely the same understanding of particular items of doctrine, order and devotion, do not apply here. Shared baptism would shed further light on the significance of these items in relation to shared eucharist.

Eucharistic celebration: transcending divisions
The divisive points in understanding the eucharist after the Reformation seemed insuperable. Memorial versus sacrifice, real presence versus spiritual presence, validly ordained ministry through apostolic succession and communion with the universal church and its universal head, the Bishop of Rome, were the obvious and significant ones. One of the most remarkable achievements of the post-Vatican II bilateral and multilateral dialogues, from England (Windsor) to Peru (Lima), has been the overcoming of so much of this division in Agreed Statements and Texts.

Roman Catholics, Orthodox and many of the Reformed

churches agree on both the memorial and sacrificial dimensions of the eucharist. Indeed they agree that the one is achieved through the other. 'Do this in memory of me' is the mandate and the means whereby Christ's sacrifice on Calvary is re-presented sacramentally on the altar. In these sacramental elements Christ, offerer and victim, becomes present in his redemptive activity on the altar and is received by the faithful.

On the meaning and origin of the ministry there is also considerable convergence although there is continuing dispute about full continuity of the ministry of a particular church with that of the early church. Apostolic succession is understood in broader terms than heretofore and the recognition by the Vatican II and later documents of the genuinely church character of post-Reformation communities, and of the value of their worship and means of salvation, opens the way to much closer relations as churches and in worship. In graceful recognition of these convergences, conversion even to the point of sharing eucharist is no longer unthinkable. The exceptions already permitted indicate that such sharing, already suggested by a fuller understanding of baptism, would make that sharing less exceptional and more nourishing for believers and believing communities.

Into your hands, Lord
The baptismal incorporation of Christians into the Body of Christ involves their incorporation into the death and resurrection of Christ, as St Paul makes clear. In that sense their lives are eucharistic, at least called to be eucharistic, by a continuous offering of themselves in love to God and neighbour. The celebration of eucharist itself is the climax and manifestation of the eucharistic life of the baptised and believing person and community. It is in this Spirit, the Spirit of God, that the believer approaches every eucharistic celebration where two or three or more are gathered together in his name to eat and drink his body and blood in memory of him. It is in this Spirit, the Spirit of Jesus, that such celebrations should welcome all who are members of Christ by baptism and seek him with a sincere heart. In this larger context, the continuing difficulties between the churches concerning the complete understanding and sharing of the eucharist do not automatically disappear, but they are considerably relativised. Generosity in sharing with those from

other churches who wish to receive communion in the Catholic Church, for example, has many gospel analogies in Jesus' feeding of the multitudes and his fellowship meals with the excluded. In conventional theological terms, it recognises these Christians' basic membership of the Body of Christ and so of Christ's church and their faith in the one Lord and in his presence in this celebration. In terms of both sacrifice and presence, the surrender of the receiving Catholic community to the faith-request of the 'outsider' seeker, is a further testimony to the presence of the self-surrendering Christ. The power of arbitrary exclusion, so typical of the princes of this world, is not without its attractions for church leaders. To protect and to witness against such power, inclusion should be the dominant church attitude and practice.

By participating in the eucharist of Orthodox, Anglican and Reformed churches, Catholics may seek to honour these communities, their faith and worship. They recognise their sacrificial remembering, their invocation by the power of the Spirit of the presence of Christ in community, word and sacrament. They seek nourishment for their own spiritual lives and bear witness with them to the world, of the reconciling work of God in the one and unique Christ.

Invitation, encouragement and preparation
The conversion of churches to one another, and of Christians to one another in Christ, which is at the heart of the process of Christian unity, is the gift of the Spirit to be completed only in the final coming of God's kingdom. In the in-between times the search for unity is pressing under the pressure of the Spirit and the needs of the times. The eucharist as expression and means of that unity should now be the focus of church engagement. Preoccupation with difficulties should yield to concentration on possibilities. Agreed Statements and occasional experiments should move to more systematic education and practice. At least this could be a millennial goal. After a millennium of Christian divisions and associated wars, some deeper transformation is called for if Christ's prayer for unity is to be taken seriously and if the world is to believe. The change of heart and mind which would be evident in the move to inviting and encouraging Christians to share eucharist could revitalise the participating churches and help overcome traditional, associated hostilities. It would loudly proclaim Jubilee and jubilation.

Invitation and encouragement have to be accompanied by profound preparation. What has been at one level achieved already in Agreed Statements, for example, has to become a basis for broader and deeper education in agreeing churches. In the past, they have been largely ignored or even hidden from the faithful lest they disturb them. The developing practices, official on the occasion of inter-church weddings, for example, or unofficial as at funerals or in other parish settings, require reflection as well as encouragement, so that they may be a source of spiritual growth for all and of offence to none. In seminaries and sermons, in adult education and theology courses, stress will be laid on the enriching possibilities of sharing the eucharist in appropriate but generously conceived circumstances.

More than theological education and reflection on pastoral practice is required in preparation for this Jubilee conversion. Common service of the poor and excluded, and co-operation in response to all the needs of God's world, including its environmental needs, are clear ways of Christian convergence en route to conversion.

Prayer and penance (repentance) are the well-tested means of conversion to God and to one another in mind and heart and behaviour. Shared prayer and repentance-reconciliation services should be a marked feature of inter-church relations in preparation for the Jubilee. When the hope for the Jubilee is a eucharistic hope, prayerful repentance and reconciliation at personal and community-church level are all the more important. Church Unity Octave Week could become a week of penitential preparation for shared eucharist on the final Sunday. Other ecumenical conferences and meetings could include a similar pattern. Inter-church couples could be invited and encouraged to share more fully and frequently in the eucharist of their respective churches, while sharing their spiritual difficulties and achievements with family, friends or broader community.

The eucharist itself as the central and exemplary Christian prayer, includes for those properly disposed the whole range of preparatory penance and instruction, reconciliation and conversion necessary to sharing in the death and resurrection of Christ, of receiving his Body and at once entering more fully into that Body. Other valuable preparatory activities should not obscure the transforming process of the eucharistic celebration itself, even for those untutored in the niceties of theology. The convergence which these and similar attitudes and activities might be expected to generate would undoubtedly lead to the deeper conversion to unity for which Jesus prayed.

CHAPTER SIX

Unopened Ground

In the first issue of *The Furrow* the founder and first editor, J. G. McGarry, spoke of opening new ground for the church in Ireland. Despite the encouraging remarks of the then Archbishop of Armagh, in a preface to that first issue, it is very doubtful if any of the episcopal or other leaders of the Catholic Church in Ireland saw the necessity or even the possibility of opening any such new ground. For them the Irish church had reached a plateau of success in education and social influence, in priestly and religious vocations for home and foreign missions, in church attendance, popular devotion and pastoral care. Innovation would be not only unnecessary but harmful. *The Furrow* never became an episcopal favourite.

Whatever new ground McGarry and his associates had in mind in 1950, the ploughing, harrowing and harvesting of the last fifty years must have greatly exceeded their expectations. In a church and a country reluctant to recognise and thank prophets and innovators, the achievement of *The Furrow* has gone largely unmarked. Perhaps the only appropriate recognition is that of its contributors and readers who have greatly increased in number and diversity in the intervening years. To be fair, the contributors have included quite a number of bishops, showing their sense of its value. It has also included leading figures in politics, the arts, the media and community work of all kinds as well as lay people, religious and priests whose voice would otherwise be rarely heard in public debate. The contributors and readers reached far beyond Ireland and Catholicism to the limits of at least the Christian churches. Ecumenical dialogue and world-mission were early concerns of the founder-editor. In that global mosaic of writers and readers resides the true monument to *The Furrow*'s first fifty years. With them we may celebrate fifty remarkably fruitful years.

Monuments and memories of past glories were never a priority with *The Furrow*. Understanding the pressures of the present might well demand further examination of the past but not in a spirit of triumph or nostalgia. As the commitment to opening new ground promised, *The Furrow* sought to read and to write the signs of the coming as well as the present times. The coming reign of God rather than departing ecclesiastical rule determined its orientation. Fifty years on, with that ecclesiastical rule in disarray and disrepute, *The Furrow* will have to be more clearly of the future. The acceleration of social and human change hastens the departure of dying or dead religious structures and practices. That departure could facilitate the inbreaking reign of God, provided there is a living and growing Christian community capable of discerning and promoting the divine dimensions of that ambiguous human progress. *The Furrow* of the future will, on the basis of its past, play a significant role in that discernment and promotion.

The Furrow *idiom: pastoral, esslesial and theological*
The Furrow began as a self-described pastoral monthly, the first of its kind in Ireland. Pastoral had a rather circumscribed meaning at that time. It dealt immediately and almost exclusively with priestly activity in the parish. That activity itself was conceived in largely sacred, sacramental and sacristy terms. Chaplain to the Legion of Mary or the Catholic Boy Scouts might qualify as pastoral but the broader involvement of so many priests in community development, in the GAA or other sporting organisations, in the local drama group or musical society, while often regarded as admirable, were not regarded as strictly speaking pastoral. *The Furrow* assumed a broader interpretation of pastoral, both in regard to the activities of ordained priests as pastors and gradually in relation to the activities of the baptised and confirmed, religious and lay. Vatican II, conceived and carried through as a pastoral Council, endorsed and transformed the original intuition of *The Furrow*. *The Furrow* joined enthusiastically in communicating the work of the Council to the Irish church and in subsequently promoting its implementation. The pastoral language and interests of *The Furrow* were renewed and deepened by the Council documents, in particular by the *Pastoral Constitution on the Church in the Modern World*.

All the major documents of Vatican II revealed a new vision of church. Pastoral the Council might be in the intent of Pope

John XXIII and other leading Council fathers such as Cardinal
Suenens, but it was in achievement equally ecclesial. The new
ecclesial vision overturned many clerical privileges and prejudices with its emphasis on church as primarily people, its recognition of separated Christian communities as sister churches, its
openness to dialogue with non-Christians and its ringing en-
dorsement of religious freedom for all. To J. G. McGarry and *The
Furrow* the new *ecclesia* of the gathered people offered fresh insights to be explored and fresh energy to explore and implement
them. The pastoral monthly was becoming an ecclesial journal
as its later subtitle, *A Journal for the Contemporary Church*, confirmed. Central to these developments was the vision of church
not only as people, but as pastoral people. All the baptised were
called to pastoral service, however diverse. Baptism was the
primary sacrament in church membership and activity, not
ordination.

Underpinning all this ecclesial and pastoral development
was a theology partly recovered from traditional sources,
particularly the scriptures and the early church theologians, and
partly discovered and developed in the face of new cultural and
political developments. The theology of the church as people of
God, rooted as it is in the scriptures and early church, was undoubtedly given a fresh impetus by the development of democracy and human rights, so fiercely resisted by some church leaders for so long. The theological acumen necessary to discern
these and other modern insights and integrate them into the
church's self-understanding did not originate in *The Furrow* or in
Ireland. Both were willing to learn in varying degrees. The early
issues of *The Furrow* avoided the conventional theological discussions of the day. Vatican II changed all that and the pages of
The Furrow began to combine the idiom and analysis of Vatican
II theology with its pastoral and ecclesial interests. *The Furrow* of
the future will be no less inclusive.

Imagined communities and the reign of God
The current widespread sense of failure to realise the high hopes
of Vatican II is due at many levels to a failure of imagination, the
very imagination which raised these hopes in the first place. The
recovery and discovery work of the Council imagined new connections with other churches and religions. It envisioned the
Catholic Church as people before hierarchy, and the liturgy as

truly the work of the believing people and not just of the priest. These were achievements of creative and imaginative scholarship, insight and prayer. The imagination at work here was not free-wheel fantasising but the committed, prayerful and Spirit-led attempt to combine imaginatively and fruitfully treasures old and new, as gift of the God who had come in Jesus Christ and of the God who was still coming in the creative and redemptive times at hand and ahead. Discerning the signs of the times is always a work of the creative and Christian imagination. Vatican II managed it confidently and superbly. The intervening years have seen a decline in that creativity and confidence. The church of the new century and millennium is more spancelled in its leadership and more frustrated and demoralised in its membership than for many a decade. Holy Spirit and Christian imagination will undoubtedly combine again to renew the church which, in the promise of Jesus, will not be allowed to pass away. When will they combine? And where? And how? That knowledge is not available to us. Ours is the task of preparing the way for the continuous coming of the Paraclete and the releasing of the Christian imagination. To that task *The Furrow* of the future will undoubtedly contribute.

In promulgating a fresh vision of the church and its mission, some Council Fathers may have believed that promulgation meant, as in law, effective realisation. Others of course, particularly in the Roman curia, interpreted the vision minimally as requiring minor and mechanical modifications to the *status quo*. Few recognised the imaginative work still to be done if the vision were not to remain a mere ideal, far from the reality of actual church structure and practice.

The ideal and image of church as people of God is scarcely discernible in the village of Ballybeg or the city of Nairobi or even the diocese of Rome. The imaginative moves which would gradually enable the baptised and believing to claim their dignity and their roles in forming an authentic community of disciples have for the most part been absent. The Sunday eucharist may have included lay readers and ministers of the eucharist but it is still priest rather than people dominated. The language and ritual remain a creaky translation from the Latin. It is all far removed from the climactic celebration of Christian loving and living heralded at the Council. Community consciousness, community structures and community practices at local, national and international levels are still largely unopened ground for the Catholic Church. *The Furrow* of the future will need further imaginative contributions from pastors and people, from people as pastors themselves in opening new ground as its preparation for a renewed church.

The rigidity of so many church structures and the dullness of so much of its language and practices are partly due to the church's inability to distinguish clearly between itself and the kingdom or reign of God, or to understand its role in discerning and promoting God's reign. Identifying church and kingdom, which sometimes happens, destroys the historical, pilgrim and relative character of the church, distorting it into a pseudo-divine, unchangeable, absolute and inevitably authoritarian institution. Power, increasingly centralised power, replaces service and gentile lording comes disguised in Jesus language. Opening up the space between church and kingdom liberates the church to open and cultivate the historical ground it has been given and in which the kingdom will emerge. The divine endowment of the church with its creative and imaginative capacities for this historical task may be analysed and categorised in various ways. The analysis and categories adopted here are intended to illuminate the future tasks of *The Furrow* and similar church enterprises.

A people: sacred and secular
The new community imagined and inaugurated by Jesus was a people bonded in faith, hope and love. The faith, hope and love were gift and call from God-made-man, from Creator become cosmic. The bonding was both sacred and secular, with Godself, with one another as children of God and as human beings, with the cosmos as divine creation and evolutionary process. The sacred as the Creator's presence and achievement could and should be distinguished from the purely human and cosmic, but cannot be finally separated. The imaginative sensitivity which would respect and explore the distinction while maintaining the unity faces acute difficulties from the religious and secular fundamentalists of today. The crudeness of some of our debates on religious and moral issues too frequently manifest these fundamentalisms. Journals such as *The Furrow*, which have displayed such sensitivity in the past, will find the sacred-secular task of communication and community-building threatened by the

spiteful soundbitery of fundamentalist factions. The positive discerning and cherishing of the sacred and the secular and their interconnections offer fresh opportunities to God's priestly people.

Seeing things as they are is, paradoxically to some people, a requirement of the Christian believer. True faith involves wonder and humility before all truth. It involves a trust in truth, a trust in the human capacity for truth, a capacity to discover and to accept. The imagined community of the future church will cherish truth from wheresoever it comes. It will as a priestly people recognise and protect the divine spark that illuminates all things seen, the sacred intrinsic to the secular, the transcendent in the immanent. In Christian tradition this divine spark, the image of God, has been recognised primarily in human beings. In practice the divine spark in other human beings, the stranger or the enemy, slaves or women, has been frequently obscured or denied. The history of Christianity's inhumanity is a history of betrayal of faith, of refusal to recognise the divine in the human other.

If the divine is not to be obscured or denied, neither is the strictly human diversity, the secular of-this-world human diversity which characterises human individuals, communities and cultures. The church's call to catholicity is a call to celebrate and to inhabit, or rather to be inhabited by this human diversity.

Imagining and promoting that kind of community is a demanding and costly undertaking. Through *The Furrow* of the future in its contribution to the catholicising of the church, a whole new range of different and neglected voices will be heard, directly and indirectly. The Christian people in all their sacred and secular diversity, and in all their different combinations of sacred and secular, must be free to speak out of their particular circumstance. Their very different ideas and experiences of the sacred, of God and prayer, of the Spirit in life and love, need to be expressed and understood. Their understanding, acceptance and rejection of particular church doctrines and structures, their attraction to other religious and spiritual visions, all these require open yet sensitive discussion if the Christian community is to grow in truthfulness and catholicity.

In cherishing the sacred, the secular has its role as context and contrast. There is no access to the Word of God without the human word, no sacramental presence of creator-redeemer without the secular realities of water and oil, of bread and wine.

Baker and wine-maker, farmer and hydrologist provide lift-off for the sacred as they perform their secular services with their own autonomous significance. The differentiation in unity of sacred and secular is a continuing task of the theological and pastoral imagination which enables disciples of Jesus the Saviour to take creation fully seriously and on its own terms. It also liberates the community of disciples to work with all who take this world seriously but who fail to recognise that the secular needs the sacred to safeguard its very secularity. That failure may in part be caused by the failure of the believing, sacred community to respect the integrity of the secular, human and cosmic. In the church of the future the interplay of sacred and secular, their mutual respect, challenge and enrichment, could open new and fertile ground.

The artistic imagination and the sacred
Artisan and artist, technician and scientist, producer and trader can therefore respect and serve the secular while leaving room for the sacred. In present-day Ireland that old-fashioned truth needs to be emphasised lest the success of so many secular projects entirely eclipse the sacred, or the defeat of so many traditional sacred projects leave the secular without any enduring value or basis. In such a situation artists in particular can play a mediating role. And many Irish artists do, although not self-consciously or directly. The best may prefer the *oratio obliqua* when it comes to value or spirit level. Derek Mahon's poem, 'A Disused Shed in County Wexford', with its echoes of the Jewish holocaust and other human horrors, Michael Longley's 'Ceasefire' published on the occasion of the first IRA ceasefire in 1994, and Tony O'Malley's painting, 'The Ghost of Clare Island', open wounds and open ground where the spirit stirs and the sacred may be discerned. And if the arrogant introductory line to Messiah XXI on Irish television, 'Music is the Messiah', recalls ancient struggles between art and religion, between humanity and the gods, it underlines a tendency of artist and priest to a self-sufficiency that denies the integrity of both art and religion, of the sacred and the secular. In the course of its half-century, *The Furrow* has engaged with the artists of the day. Usually this has been with those artists more explicitly religious in their work. Such artists as painter Patrick Pye, sculptor Imogen Stuart, architects like Richard Hurley or the late Liam McCormack, and

priest-poets like Pádraic Daly, Paul Murray and Pat O'Brien and many others, contribute more directly to distinguishing and uniting the holy and the beautiful, the sacred and the secular. Their mediating role is as a minority within the artistic community itself as well as between it and the religious or priestly people. It is the artists as a body in their varying degrees of religious belief and unbelief who offer a distinct route to the creative and healing spirit active in the world. A more systematic attention to their work in search of renewal in the spirit will be part of the church's and *The Furrow's* future task.

In line with its established tradition, *The Furrow* will be concerned above all with the holy and the beautiful in worship and liturgy, in the words and the symbols, in the forms and the rituals, in the settings and the places, in the music and the movement. There is no reason why the prayers of the faithful should be usually so banal, why the offertory processions should be so dull, why the kiss of peace should be so embarrassing or why preacher and congregation have never the creative time or energy for a truly transforming sermon. Should the traditional homily notes be replaced by the occasional lengthy sermon, rich in the rhetoric of the Christian and contemporary classics, if only as a corrective to the casual homiletic chatter too many people have to endure every Sunday? Other sacraments and liturgies call for similar renewal in grace-giving form.

And who are the artistic helpers who directly or indirectly could help reunite holiness and beauty in our liturgies? What would theatrical producers and directors like Michael Colgan and Patrick Mason have to offer? And the dramatists themselves whose art has its own liturgical roots? And the poets and the painters, to a liturgical world in which the verbal and the visual have to match the transcendent? Far too much for one journal to undertake, but it could give a lead to a church whose sense of the beautifully holy has been lost and whose other resources in publication and education, in prayer and pastoral care, could help recover it.

The enduring prophetic
The holy and the beautiful, characteristic of God's reign/kingdom, may well be undermined by the unjust behaviour of those charged with protecting the holy and promoting the divine reign. This prophetic theme marked Jesus' own preaching and

promotion of the kingdom. It has been an enduring feature of the Christian community as individual and communal prophetic voices summoned the church to the kingdom works of freedom, justice and reconciliation/peace. For much of the last century, especially the second half (*The Furrow* half), the church has raised prophetic voices in the cause of human rights and freedoms, of justice and peace. There have been lamentable lapses and silences also, not least in the Europe of the holocaust. In recent decades, however, the preaching and the promotion of the kingdom values have been fairly persistent and consistent around the globe. In Ireland episcopal statements and church commissions, like that of Justice and Peace at home and Trócaire in the developing world, as well as individual church members and voluntary organisations, have preached and promoted justice in society. The work and witness of the Society of St Vincent de Paul, of Sean Healy and Brigid Reynolds, of Sister Stan, Peter McVerry and Harry Bohan, are known and admired throughout Ireland. Their work and that of many others, lay and religious, may be partially obscured by the recent church scandals but the work goes on and the prophetic witness remains.

The Furrow has attended regularly to these prophetic voices and activities. Increased prominence might be given not only to recognised social justice issues but also to care of the environment and perhaps to the personal and pastoral challenges associated with genetically modified foods, food security, genetic engineering and human cloning. The scientific shaping of our world is largely unopened ground for many Christians and must become their immediate concern. No one journal with limited resources can take on all the challenges of modern society. *The Furrow* will have to focus on those which are within the interest and capacity of its writers and readers. It may never neglect a truly prophetic church voice but it may seek to attract those voices which address the more urgent of its interests.

Clearly within *The Furrow*'s interests are the issues of freedom, justice and reconciliation within the church itself. Much has been written about the unjust treatment of awkward and prophetic voices within the church by Roman curial and other church officials. Bishops, theologians and pastoral workers, clerical, religious and lay, have been harassed and punished without justice at least being seen to be done. The climate of fear, suspicion and distrust which these actions have generated is doing great damage to the mission of the church and seriously damaging its credibility as a kingdom witness in the world to the values of freedom, justice and peace. The prophetic imagination in the church will have to be engaged not just in denouncing these practices, but in devising new structures and practices which will prevent such injustices recurring.

In his recent book, Archbishop John Quinn (formerly of San Francisco) took very seriously Pope John Paul II's invitation in his encyclical *Ut Unum Sint,* to suggest ways of renewing the papacy so that it could more clearly, effectively and lovingly exercise its ministry of unity to all Christians. Catholic cynics and prophets might say that it needs first to be renewed in the exercise of its ministry of unity to all Catholics and especially those who have been reading the signs of the times as instructed by Vatican II. These and all Catholics have to move beyond mere criticism to developing new procedures and structures for a more just and participatory church. Indeed the church can never become more just without becoming more participatory. While repeating the mantra, 'the church is not a democracy', many church leaders forget to add that it is not by divine institution a monarchy or an oligarchy either, appearances it too often offers to the questioning among its own. And while borrowing the trappings and practices of earlier but now superseded political structures, sometimes against the spirit of its crucified Lord, it refuses to learn from the more humane and just practices of the modern democratic state. Whatever the limitations of that state in theory and practice, and they are many, its separation of powers, its participatory structures and practices and its constitutional/legal protection of human rights offer the best available guarantee of respect for human dignity and integral human development in a just society, something popes and bishops have recently and frequently averred. That it might provide a model for the reform of church structures and practices, as earlier political models did, and without undermining Christ's original endowment, has not struck home at papal, curial or episcopal level yet. Of course the groundwork has not been done in theology or local pastoral practice which would begin to liberate minds and transform attitudes of fear and control into ones of trust and collaboration, a large tract of unopened ground.

From prophetic justice to Christian faith?

From the Hebrew prophets through Jesus to the church of the new millennium, faith in Yahweh/God has inspired and challenged believers in pursuit of justice. In what many regard, at least in the western world, as a post-Christian era, the pursuit of justice without faith is a widespread phenomenon. Of more interest to *The Furrow* readers and writers may be the new reality of people inspired by Christian motives to work for justice who subsequently see no need for faith or certainly no need for church. Indeed some who were moved by church teaching to work for justice come to see church as obstacle rather than support. This has happened to women workers for justice, no doubt affected by their perception of church as unfavourable to justice for women within its own ambit. But it is true of many men as well who are conscious of injustice and oppression within while fighting it without. The lack of justice in the church undermines its apostolate and its apostles for justice in the world.

There may be, however, another dynamism at work whereby those who work for justice, Christian or post-Christian, may find their way through the justice-seeking and peace-making to the prophetic beatitude-giver and his God. In the decades ahead first evangelisation may be in terms of the promotion of freedom, justice and peace on their own terms. This may be for many the first access to the transcendent, to the God of Jesus Christ. It may also be their last. There can be no guarantee of moving from the commitment to justice for its own sake to faith recognition. Yet it will be a major pastoral task for the future to honour justice-seeking as God-seeking, to encourage and to form alliances with the justice-seekers, to respect their integrity and not try to manipulate them. The prayerful, pastoral and theological exploration of justice will still be necessary for the fuller meaning it may offer justice and for the fuller understanding it may offer Christian faith. From faith to justice and back to faith, and more challengingly from justice to faith and back to justice, will involve fruitful hermeneutical circles.

Embodied wisdom

The biblical categories of the priestly and the prophetic have a third partner in wisdom. If in simplified terms the priestly concerns recognition of the holy, the prophetic that of the just, then wisdom reflects the gift of good judgement in a confusing world. In the fragmented, even chaotic life with which so many Christians are confronted in church and society today, the gift and practice of sound judgement are repeatedly required. Sound judgement is not necessarily cautious judgement, still less fearful judgement, the kind of judgement which has paralysed so many church leaders and enterprises in recent decades. It is the courageous judgement that set the Creator-God on the wonderful but parlous journey of creation in the first place. And the even more courageous judgement that led to incarnation, from birth in a stable to crucifixion as a criminal on a cross. It is the kind of judgement that led the first apostles to martyrdom and the other great saints to the equivalent self-sacrificing love of God and neighbour. On a suitably reduced scale it is the kind of courageous judgement that led to the founding of *The Furrow*. In an increasingly fearful church, to help liberate that church *The Furrow* will need to renew its courage and its judgement. The incarnate divine wisdom seeks fresh and courageous outlets beyond or even through the fearful men of little faith who often fill influential pastoral positions.

The courage and the wisdom which church and humanity need bear the sign of the cross and not the insignia of the powers of this world or of a former one. The church of the Crucified seeks to heal and include, not to condemn and punish. It seeks to learn from and live with. It searches for ways to reconciliation rather than for means of self-protection. A developed sacrament of reconciliation, for example, provided it was mutually forgiving between sinners in search of sainthood and not another exercise of clerical power, could be an effective embodied expression of courageous church wisdom. Such wisdom and its various embodiments could have a transforming effect on the present stagnant ecumenical situation. It could offer healing inclusion to the many hurt and alienated by church attitudes and activities, as Bishop Willie Walsh's pilgrimage through his diocese suggested. It would begin to break out of the stalemates reached on the care of, and inclusion of, Christians in unrecognised marital relationships as well as the care and inclusion of gay and lesbian Christians. It would bear witness to the destructiveness of our prison system. It would enter into necessary and useful alliances with all the justice-seekers and peace-makers. From the self-surrendering wisdom of the Cross it would prepare for resurrection, for new human life in a new millennium, for the further inbreaking of the reign of God. This embodied wisdom can only be fully and properly expressed and lived in the whole body of believers, the Body of Christ.

A pastoral journey in an internet world
The optimistic techno-boffins and the pessimistic book-lovers express hopes/fears that the era of the book and journal, indeed of all the print media, is coming to an end. Accelerating techno-logical developments in communication during the last decade should make anyone hesitate about predicting future possibili-ties. *The Furrow*, like all publications, benefits from the advances in fax and e-mail as it takes its own place in the world of the Internet with its own website. The advantages in communica-tion and production of material are clear. The broader dissemin-ation which a website offers could give the work of *The Furrow* a much larger audience and consequently greater influence. One might ask, however, how pastoral this influence will continue to be and how intellectually, morally and spiritually nourishing work prepared for and received only on the Internet will re-main. The personal and community dimensions of communic-ation, education and care may not be finally handed over to machines. And the extended, reflective analysis which so many human issues require may still be best achieved and received through the book in the hand. As it faces the challenge of the IT revolution, *The Furrow* and its print companions may have to make serious adjustments, but the basic Christian mission and human means will retain their own value.

At the beginning of a new century and a new millennium, *The Furrow* has much to celebrate and to hope for. This relates closely to its founding momentum, to serve the church by ac-knowledging its achievement and resources, criticising its weak-nesses and preparing for its reform. Unsurprisingly, a golden ju-bilee reflection on *The Furrow* has been preoccupied with the human successes and failures as well as with the divine promises which continue to characterise the community of Jesus' disci-ples. Adapting Séamus Heaney's title, 'Opened Ground', and in-spired by the ground opened over its fifty years, *The Furrow* can recognise that it has much unopened ground to cultivate. And to add to the adaptations, *floreat ut floreat*.

CHAPTER SEVEN

A Communal Hope

Phil Dunne's article in the September 2003 issue of *The Furrow* must be one of the most moving and disturbing that journal has ever published. Her account of why and how she left the church after all it had meant to her and all that she had contributed to it, leaves some of those still clinging to the wreckage with serious questions to ask and to answer. Many who remain may dismiss the disturbing side, especially in so far as it focuses on women in the church, but they can hardly be untouched by the pain of a woman who faced, as she believed, with imminent death felt bound to refuse the usual consolations of Sunday Mass and community worship. The clarity imposed by such a threat exposes the authenticity and courage of her testimony and how deeply disturbing it may be for others. This deeply disturbed other who shares many of Phil Dunne's frustrations (what an inadequate word!) has to labour anew to discover why he and many others remain. Out of courage or cowardice, careerism or complacency? Commitment or indecision? Hope (of the future church) or despair (of the present world)? Or the ambiguity of so many overlapping reasons and counter-reasons? All rendered the more ambiguous because Phil Dunne herself clearly remains a woman of Christian faith, hope and charity, of sacrament and community, even if she no longer sees herself as a member of the institutional Catholic Church.

In her succinct summary she says: 'I have moved away from an institutional church that excludes the vast majority of members from decision making, that seeks to maintain itself even at the cost of ignoring the Spirit, and that pays only lip service to women. I have moved away, not for such reasons but because I see no possibility of change. I move away as a signal that I can no longer condone such behaviour by my presence. I move away in the hope that my move multiplied by many may bring about the collapse of the present structures.'

The first high-profile Catholic theologian to leave the institutional Catholic Church after Vatican II was the Westminster priest Charles Davis in 1967. He gave as his primary reason the corruption in the church, as exemplified in particular in church authority's handling of contraception. In a brilliant and sympathetic critique of Davis's leaving, Herbert McCabe OP wrote in an editorial in *New Blackfriars* that such corruption was no reason to leave then as the church had always been corrupt. This seemed very convincing to many at the time although not to Mc Cabe's religious and episcopal superiors. He was suspended from his priestly faculties (for a week) and as editor (for several years). It is doubtful if his response would persuade so many today, least of all perhaps Phil Dunne. As she points out, too many hopes have been dashed recently and too many more shattering examples of corruption, and its bosom companion cover-up, have emerged in the Irish and in the international church. And yet …

An outsider could never hope to understand fully the complex reasons of a decision such as Phil Dunne's, still less presume to refute them. However, reflecting seriously on such a decision may provoke the kind of self-examination which could confirm one's own commitment or persuade one to follow her lead and contribute to that collapse which she believes is necessary to renew the church. Self-examination is always difficult. In this matter it is also dangerous for somebody who has lived almost a whole life within the structures, if not always by their dictates.

In his devotional but still powerful poem, 'The Blessed Virgin Compared to the Air We Breathe', Gerard Manley Hopkins offers a telling insight into the multiple ecclesial, cultural and social atmospheres in which believing people live. Like the air we breathe, the faith and church atmosphere, the political atmosphere, the secular/non-religious cultural atmosphere and the socio-economic atmosphere, all these we inhale and exhale unconsciously. Even as these atmospheres change, and they have been changing rapidly in Ireland, we fail to notice until there is either a serious pollution problem or a significant clearing of the air. Of the four atmospheres listed, and there might be more, one may be dominant in a particular individual or society at a particular time but they are all usually intermingled in harmonious and/or conflicting ways. By concentrating on, say, the faith-church atmosphere at any time it is possible to gauge how far it is polluted or clean and how far it is influenced by, say, the polit-

ical, the broader cultural or the socio-economic and vice versa,
and how far these three are influenced by the faith-church atmosphere. More obvious recent interminglings included those
of Catholicism and nationalism, Protestantism and unionism. It
took thirty years of violence in Northern Ireland properly to reveal the mutual polluting effects of religion and politics in
Ireland. And the revelation and the cleansing remedies are far
from complete.

All this by way of showing what tangled lives we lead, how
difficult it is to isolate the church-faith dimension of these lives.
Perhaps the attempt is misguided and the church-faith dimension cannot be isolated in any pure way when dealing with a
community believing in both creation and incarnation as well as
in redemption and resurrection. It is in and through the cosmos
and the biosphere, and through human beings in relationship, in
community and in history that human faith in God is established. The obscurity of that faith generally derives from the
opaqueness of the material world and not from any necessary
conflict between matter and spirit. In the Christian story, such
dualism is inadmissible. In human and Christian history the
opaqueness and fragility of humans as inspirited-matter have
led often to the rupturing of both divine-human relationships
and human-human relationships. The fuller divine-human engagement in Jesus Christ has provided the healing and transforming grace to overcome such ruptures, the grace to be mediated through the community of Jesus' disciples. Unfortunately
now as in Jesus' time, their cowardice and power-seeking have
prevented this community and its leaders from exercising their
mediating/reconciling role after the example and in the Spirit of
Jesus. For Phil Dunne and so many others, church leaders, episcopal and clerical, are failing to lead a healing, reconciling and
transforming community.

All this is well known and frequently, too frequently perhaps, rehearsed in public and in private. The struggles for reform, in which Phil Dunne with so many other disillusioned
women and men, have honourably engaged, still continue.
However, they seem to yield such nugatory results despite good
intentions and serious efforts that a critical evaluation of their
goals, motivating forces and methods seems overdue. As Anne
Codd pointed out at the Annual Conference of the Priests of
Ireland, the conflict over the implementation of Vatican II may,

given its apparently irreconcilable interpretations, be left aside at least for the moment. The structural reforms outlined by Donal Dorr at the same conference, and published in the October issue of *The Furrow*, are undoubtedly valuable if not easily implemented in the present church atmosphere. Indeed in the current intermingling and mutual pollution of religious and secular atmospheres mentioned earlier, it is difficult to know what would clear the Irish air politically, economically or ecclesially. Without seeking excuses, but in search of accurate diagnosis and eventual healing, it has to be admitted that the Irish church and its leaders are victim as well as cause of many of the ills afflicting Irish society.

The church as moral community
Criticism of the church, its leaders and general membership usually concentrate on their moral failings. Phil Dunne's criticisms are basically in this tradition. In failing to listen to the concerns of their people and in persisting with unjust treatment of women members, church leaders have exposed their moral failure and forfeited the trust of many. That this is not a new phenomenon but a long-standing weakness of church leaders is not an acceptable excuse for those immediately involved and offended. In the last decade this moral failure has been most dramatically exemplified in the scandal of clerical sex abuse and paedophilia and their associated cover-ups, and all against a background of a church presuming to exert moral leadership for the whole society and particularly vocal and demanding on issues of sexual morality. In a society in which there is at least a confusion if not a collapse of moral values, the role of the church leaders and members in teaching and embodying a moral way of life needs careful scrutiny and serious renewal. 'Physician heal thyself' has a disturbing ring for would-be preachers of Christian morality today.

There can be no doubt that the disciples of Jesus Christ are called individually and as a community to a morally good way of life. The primacy of charity, the Sermon on the Mount, the example as well as the teaching of Jesus himself and the teaching-authority and lifestyle of the first Christian community bear ample witness to this. And while many of the most serious crises and divisions in the history of the church turned on questions of doctrine, there was always or almost always a sub-text of moral failure. This was clearly true in the run-up to the critical divisions of the Reformation. In its efforts to move beyond the older polarisations of Reformation and Counter-Reformation, Vatican II made its own the traditional cry, *ecclesia semper reformanda*, the church is always in need of reform or renewal. In more biblical and realistic terms, that might be rendered as the church, its leaders and members are always in need of repentance, *metanoia*, a radical conversion of heart, mind and behaviour. For the church in history is a communion of sinners and only in hope a communion of saints. In church as in so many other spheres of human living, hope and history seldom rhyme. This theme will return in considering the church as eschatological community and its relationship to the reign of God.

The call to repentance, involving a call to a better self, implies not only the potential for such a better self but some of the ideals and practices which such a self would involve. The teaching and example of Jesus provide the template for this better self for community and individual disciple. Despite its recurring moral and intellectual failures, the community of disciples has developed its understanding and practice of Jesus' teaching and example in widely different historical circumstances and in ways which enable it constantly to evaluate and reform its moral performance. The values and virtues, the attitudes and practices which Jesus modeled, have persisted in the church's conscious or at least its sub-conscious life as judge and stimulus at even its worst moments, to emerge perhaps in the eccentric voices of fools and prophets as a reminder of the prophetic, loving and creative foolishness of the God of Jesus Christ. In face of the antigentilism of some early Christians, as in the face of the antisemitism of so many later ones, there have been prophetic opponents from Paul of Tarsus to Maximilian Kolbe. The deterioration of just war into medieval crusade and on into the horrors of modern war has frequently evoked Christian protest, if seldom as forceful as the recent Vatican opposition to the war on Iraq. As these sketchy examples illustrate, the church's moral record has by its own founder's standards always been mixed so that repentance and forgiveness are in constant demand.

How to preach and present authentically and effectively the moral demands of the gospel in the light of its own past and present performance is a continuing challenge to the church and its leaders. Only in the mode of humility and repentance should it dare to undertake the task. Yet it may not shirk announcing the moral implications of the good news of salvation, giving priority of course to the good news aspect and remembering Jesus' own admonition: 'Repent and believe the good news.' Indeed it is the good news for preacher and preached to, that the forgiving God makes the first move. As grace anticipates achievement, so forgiveness anticipates repentance and yet that forgiving move of God is only completed by human acceptance in repentance. A genuinely humble and repentant church may confidently proclaim the moral demands of the good news. A resistant and self-righteous church may not. In Phil Dunne's experience, and that of others too, many church leaders are resisting the voices of lay people through whom the Spirit may be speaking, bringing the further truth which Jesus promised in his farewell speech to the disciples. The power-temptations of authority too easily lead to deafness and blindness of the kind so sharply criticised by Jesus in the religious leaders of his time.

It is clearly impossible to discuss the church as moral (and immoral) community without considering it in its relationship to Jesus Christ and his God, which at once establishes and undermines its authority. Without that relationship in history and practice it has no special claim to moral authority; given that relationship, its moral weaknesses and lack of repentance appear to undermine its claim. As it proclaims and seeks justice and peace, truth and freedom in a spirit of love and forgiveness for all, the church is true to its Christian vocation and despite inevitable lapses offers effective witness as moral community in the world. The moral achievement and witness is derived from the presence and power of Christ in the church's grace-filled role as Body of Christ. The achievement and witness in turn are directed to the development of the reign or kingdom of God inaugurated and promised by Jesus Christ. In situations of apparently serious moral failure by church leaders particularly, authentic believers in the God of Jesus Christ may be called to sharp prophetic criticism of such failure, and indeed *in extremis* to the prophetic distancing of themselves from such leaders and their institutional activities. Phil Dunne would not be alone in this, now or in the past, and she would not thereby forfeit her membership of the Body of Christ or her engagement with the reign of God. How she and others might proceed to enrich that Body and promote that kingdom will vary with the individual, but in true Christian spirit they will seek the conversion of both the failing leaders and of themselves to a deeper understanding and living of the Body of Christ. This does not involve any easy resignation to the failures of the leaders as the prophetic critics perceive them, but a persistent and painful attempt to ensure truth and justice where they have, for example as women, experienced the untruth and injustice of people in authority playing games with them. Hopes for such moral conversion may ebb and flow but they are not finally determined by the good faith or good will of the protagonists, their personal moral fibre. The church in its continuing moral weakness is always more than a moral community even when it appears to its critics within and without to be less, as it most certainly has been in many places and at many stages during the clerical abuse scandals.

A sacramental community
Much of the stress and tension associated with the church is due to its 'between' status and its lack of awareness, understanding or acceptance of this fragile condition. As Body of Christ it shares in his 'betweeness', his mediating role between humanity and God but without the stabilising character of the personal incarnate God, of him who was without sin. In this 'betweenness' the church as community may be tempted to think that the perfection of the God-man is already its own. Historic periods of arrogance and corruption, of self-righteousness and oppression have seen church leaders and members identify themselves in an eventually blasphemous way with the divine in Christ, at the expense of their own frail and sinful humanity. Invoking another 'betweeness' characteristic of the church, that between history and the final reign of God, a further temptation may be discerned, that of identifying the historical community of believers with that final kingdom. And so it has been in the many periods and guises of 'Constantinianism', when church leaders wielded the 'sword of spiritual power' alongside or superior to 'the sword of temporal (imperial/state) power'. The lessons of the Inquisition are painful reminders of the worst of such failures, although there have been many (milder) examples ever since. A healthy and humbling reminder of the church's real situation derives from the 'betweeness' which von Balthasar emphasises: church and humanity live between Good Friday and Easter Sunday; in the half-life and half-light between the death of Jesus and the resurrection of Christ.

The 'betweeness' is not a static one, with church or humanity stranded in a no-man's or no-God's land. Dynamic interactions between God and humanity, between kingdom and church, between life and death are continuously at work in ways only partially recognisable. In word and sacrament, in works of charity and lives of holiness, in a community of faith, hope and love as well as of sin, the trinitarian God of Creator, Saviour and Sanctifier expresses the inner divine dynamic through created and human forms. Jesus Christ as sacrament of God, effective sign of God's presence and power; the community of disciples as sacrament of Jesus Christ, effective sign of his presence and power in the Spirit which is given to us; these are the trinitarian ways of Emmanuel, of God with us.

This tortuous attempt to focus the presence and power of the divine within the created, human and sinful, within the church, may reinforce rather than relieve the difficulties of Phil Dunne, her sisters and brothers. As there is no direct access to God for humanity in history, the tortuousness of the Holy Saturday way (to adapt von Balthasar) involves the darkness and doubt which faith and sacrament can only partly remove. The risk of faith, the fragility of believer and church leader make for a very imperfect, unfinished and untidy faith-community. Belonging to such a community is by turns illuminating and disillusioning, transforming and frustrating. Members must be prepared for leadership failure; leaders for members' anger. In the perilous journey by the half-light of faith, leaders and members must be repentant, accepting and forgiving. And it may not always be clear who the members or even the effective leaders are. Prophets come in various guises and with varying degrees of authority. Members' faith may outrun the current orthodoxy, as it did with religious freedom and ecumenism in the recent past, and may well do with the ordination of women in the near future. Certainly, as Karl Rahner was well aware, heresy is not so neatly packaged in a living faith-community and the mixture of true beliefs, mistaken beliefs, doubt and unbelief which characterises so many church members may be redeemed and transformed by trust in the community's abiding Spirit of loving truth. Trusting the Spirit may take leaders beyond their narrower views on such questions as the role of women in the church at least to accepting the good and indeed true faith of their critics, and so recognising them as authentic church members, while the same trust may enable these who disagree with certain leadership positions and practices to see themselves as faithful to Christ's church and willing to share in its sacramental celebrations. This would apply to a wide range of believers at present alienated or excluded from the sacramental life, such as couples in non-juridical marriage unions. Should these and many in similar situations be excluded despite their faith, hope and love from the sacraments, what happens to the rest of us in our sinfulness and fragile beliefs? And how far is such an excluding church a true sacrament of the including, healing and forgiving Jesus Christ?

An eschatological community
A transcendent God allows only for sacramental or symbolic communication. A transhistorical God is fully available only beyond history, at the eschaton. In that sense, in its reach towards final communion with God, the church is an eschatological community, a community of hope. As already noted, this recognition of its incompleteness should prevent the church from making an idol of itself by identifying itself with the kingdom. In its divine endowment and responsive human holiness it is an anticipation and sign/sacrament of the kingdom. In its failures it is challenged to remember that it is a movement *towards* rather an arrival *at*. Like any human and communal movement, its members find their roles, their responsibilities and their attachments variable and both confused and confusing. For example, what kind of leaders should bishops be? Saints? And what kind of saints? Prophets? For whom? Against whom? Preachers and teachers? Out of what knowledge and experience? Single presidents of the eucharist with what kind of assistance and assistants? Symbol of unity for the local church in communion with other local churches and with Rome, or local franchise holders for the multinational centred in Rome? Administrators or animators? And how does one tell which or which combination of these is suitable and working in a particular time and place? Above all, who decides their suitability and how? All of these questions have received different answers at least in practice at different times and in different places, some answers satisfactory, others far from. And bishops are only a tiny percentage of the church's members, if the most obvious ones today. Similar and further questions might be asked about the much larger number of priests and religious, still just a tiny church minority. At the

basic level of the community-church the thousands of millions of the believing and baptised would pose endless questions which may be beyond formulation let alone answer. So the present movement towards the kingdom, together with its past and future formations, should be generous with its boundaries and welcoming of the gifts of all the faithful, not just of the 'party faithful', but of the partly faithful, which is in fact all of us, bishops, priests, religious and lay people, always in need of being sustained, forgiven and transformed by the in-breaking God,

God's pilgrim people on their discipleship way to the New Jerusalem do not enjoy a detailed route map. The call of God to the way of discipleship, to seek the fullness of humanity for self and others in the final kingdom, is a call to loving creativity. The resources of moral empowerment and freedom, of divine word and sacrament for person and community enable the constant discovery of new and true ways but they do not guarantee the avoidance of new or old false ways. The history of the church has never been that of straight-line progress towards the *eschaton*, the final divine goal. Even now it may be taken for granted that, from the highest authority in the church to the simplest disciple, mistakes in policy and behaviour, in good or bad conscience, are being made. How present policies or individual judgements on liturgical language, on women's ordination, on a particular war as just or indeed on the justice of any war, may appear one hundred years on, or more significantly at the *eschaton*, must at least give everybody from Pope John Paul and Joseph Ratzinger to Phil Dunne and her church-going friend pause. And these are only a tiny sample of the questions which the church as moral and sacramental community, in its unfinished condition and eschatological orientation, must continue to consider fairly and prayerfully.

The unfinished nature of the church, its necessary historical condition, is always a source of joy and grief, grief at the attendant failure and pain, joy at the creative possibilities to which Christians are called and gracefully empowered. The joy and grief, to paraphrase Vatican II, are all the more intense in that the achievements and creative possibilities, the failures and refusals of grace and possibility, affect not only the church community itself but the whole human community for which the church bears some responsibility in that human community's journey to its final destiny in the one God. Rejoicing and regretting, repentant and reforming, these must be the constant attributes of the community of disciples as they wrestle with the inheritance of history, the possibilities and frustrations of the present and the unknowns of the future. The risks involved are obvious. What can any one person, baptised or ordained, parishioner or bishop, hope to achieve and at what cost to faith and hope and love, to personal integrity and peace of mind, should she continue the struggle, within or without the community? That is finally for individual disciples to assess and decide. In the assessment and decision as in the struggle, they need more sensitive support from the rest of the community in whatever relationship to church the struggling one now deems necessary to adopt. In her present honourable decision, Phil Dunne should be esteemed and supported by the wider believing community as should the many hesitant, doubtful, angry or alienated who are excluded or are excluding themselves for reasons open to debate in an unfinished, historical church, always partly sinful and so partly unfaithful church. In the movement towards the Father's house there may also be many mansions or at least many temporary shelters for those who may need a rest from the loud-speaker directions of the main movement. The Jesus of the last journey to Jerusalem, or still more of the Way of the Cross, would surely approve.

PART THREE

In Morality

CHAPTER EIGHT

Friendship, Sexuality and Marriage

For all the sexual liberation and licence of the Western world in the last century, many even of the liberated are still ill at ease with their bodies and their sexuality. From the prudish to the promiscuous, from the flaunting to the repressed, there may emanate a sense of dismay and sometimes of terror in face of bodily and sexual turbulence, one's own or another's. Without dwelling on the many abusive sexual practices of the day and their violent and commercial brutalities, it is important that more attention is paid by Christians, married and single, academic and lay to God-given bodily beauty and sexuality and their creative potential as well as their destructive possibilities. For Catholic Christians at least this creative potential in its sacramental realisation has a holy-making dimension which is indeed rooted in creation itself. 'Male and female he created them. In the image of God he created them.' In recognition of Professor Lawlor's own fine contribution to the whole theology of marriage as sacrament, as holy-making, I offer these reflections on marriage considered as friendship as well as sexual communion under the broad rubric of 'Vulnerable to the Holy'. I take for granted the more scholarly treatment of 'Friendship and Marriage' in Professor Lawlor's recent book, *Marriage and the Catholic Church*.

Basic to human bodiliness and its beauty is its vulnerability. In its contact with the world through the famous five senses, the human body and person is vulnerable to other bodily beings, including of course human beings. Sensitive to other bodily beings would be the more usual expression but 'vulnerable' carries important overtones of the painful openness and the possibility of hurt which all such encounters involve. The eye can bear only so much light, the heart only so much love and humankind only so much reality.

Friendship and vulnerability

On the night that Jesus acclaimed his disciples as friends, no longer servants but friends, one of them betrayed him, their leader denied him and all the other disciples deserted him except John, the beloved disciple, his mother and some of his other women disciples-friends. In calling his disciples friends, Jesus was revealing in some ways the climax of creation-incarnation. Of course humans were created out of love and for love, for love of the Creator, love of one another and love of self, not in some self-regarding, selfish way but as cherishing and caring for that God-given (bodily) being. Yet that the Creator God should become human, a bodily creature, and should enter into the give and take of human friendship to the point of being betrayed and deserted and beyond that to laying down his life for these and all his potential human friends and betrayers, all of humanity, remains barely credible.

The personal bonding, spirit-infused and embodied, which constitutes friendship is one of the adornments of human community. Even if the claim that one would rather betray one's country than one's friends is cynical in intention, and the corruption of friendship in political and commercial cronyism has become a common disease, the loyalty and affection of friendship and the self-sacrifice which frequently accompanies them, can be a beacon of light and a continuing source of hope for people threatened with darkness and despair.

At such profound level, friendship is not that common and never easy. Even allowing for the human weakness of Jesus' disciples-friends, in truth a universal human weakness, discerning the potential richness and potential destructiveness of any particular friendship or of human friendship in general is a daunting task. The experience of living and broken friendships provide many immediate insights, although in the reflective theological mode of this essay more systematic analysis is called for. As the mode is theological the analysis will have to struggle with both the divine and human dimensions of friendship.

In the typical case, human friends form a unity or community while retaining their distinctiveness. The distinctiveness is more accurately described as difference between two people, the irreducibility of the one to the other. In sharper terms still they could be seen, despite their bonds of unity, as utterly other and indeed, as they were in the beginning, still to a large extent strangers to one another. The difference, the otherness, the strangeness is at once the basis for their bonding in friendship and the threat to its survival. All strangers who become friends, and only strangers can, like spouses at first meeting, parents and newborn children, all the friends acquired over a lifetime, are always at risk of fresh and hostile estrangement. Life is littered with broken marriages, broken families, broken friendships. The fragility of marriage, family and friendship is notorious. Yet friendship endures sometimes heroically, although it may in many instances be in need of repair, even running repairs. The multiplicity of counselling services is some witness to that, but they only succeed, when they do, because of the resilient capacity and continuing need of people for friendship, love and community.

Strangers in the half-light
Tracking personal relations from casual acquaintance to close friendship to marriage and parenthood may follow diverse routes. The historical development of any particular friendship or marriage can lead to fascinating questions and sometimes disquieting or elusive answers. When did we first meet? What did we see in each other? What kept us together or (nearly) drove us apart? Conversations of this kind are the privilege of all relationships. A different kind of approach is adopted here as a more general analysis seeks to understand some of the major underlying characteristics of how humans may relate to one another and eventually to their God.

All begin as strangers. The newborn is stranger to her parents as they are to her. More radically, human beings were in that novel sense also strangers to their Creator-God as God was and is to them. The act of creation or better, in terms of the Genesis poetic narrative as well as in terms of evolution's scientific narrative, the process of creation is a story of emerging strangers. Creation, divine or human, as alienation or estrangement may not be the more usual description, yet it is essential to maintaining the individuality and distinctiveness of the created. For human creatures the alienation, the separation as an other (*alius*), is crucial to human and divine autonomy, to the theism of the Jewish, Christian and Islamic traditions. Only within that context of alienation, separation and autonomy are the free relationships of friendship/love possible. The language of alien-

ation itself seems foreign to that of love and friendship, suggest-
ing rather their antithesis in enmity. However, it is useful in
stressing the depth of difference (a softer term) critical to eventual depth of unity as well as attending to the fragility of all
human love relations, constantly threatened by hostile alienation as in the crucial case of Jesus and his friends.

More significantly the alienation or otherness of human persons and of human persons and their God reveals that all loving
relations have, as it is said, to be worked at, to be built on. They
are always in process like creation itself. And that process is always also a process of overcoming alienation, of reconciliation.
In the great reconciliation story of God and God's creation the
divine creative energies continually reveal and integrate the developing otherness/difference of every aspect of that creation.
Alienation and reconciliation constitute a kind of dialectic of
true creation. Without the simultaneous exercise of reconciliation it would not be one creation or God's creation. And for
every human creature within that divine world, the sharing in
God's work of creating and reconciling is her glory.

In images which parallel that of alienating and reconciling,
friendship may be explored in terms of darkness and light, the
darkness and light which interacted in the Genesis story and in
the passion-resurrection stories. The dark stranger aptly describes every human being newly encountered. In a developing
relationship the darkness is partially banished as the light of the
other's life emerges. In even the closest friendship or marriage
some darkness remains and may at times intensify. The other
never becomes fully transparent for the very obvious reason that
there is more to everybody than meets the eye, even the most
familiar and practised eye. That more could on occasion be
threat but it is also promise and potential of more light, of more
to be loved. It is hardly necessary to labour the analogy between
human relations understood in these terms and divine-human
relations as recorded at least in the Jewish and Christian scriptures. The light of divine self-revelation is the context for divine-
human relations in the history of Israel as in the person of Christ,
light of the world, the light shining in the darkness, the darkness
which did not comprehend or eventually master it (John 1).

In certain circumstances the darkness may prevail between
friends. Reconciliation and creation are no longer operative.
Trust is destroyed and love embittered. That is the dangerous

world of human relationships as between persons and even classes of persons, ethnic groups or whole nations. The grand social breakdown is called war. Yet the creative, reconciling Spirit, the Holy Spirit is still at work in the broken personal relationship as it is in the destructive enmities of war. The sheer hurt and vulnerability of disappointed personal loving may open to the healing presence of the holy where that holy has been experienced and is recalled from the first now broken loving. In the dramatic falling in love, as well as in the steady growth of friendship, the primacy of the other transcends in theological terms to the primacy of the Ultimate Other. That Other in its very linguistic development (Hebrew *qadosh*, Greek *hagios*, Latin *sanctus*) refers to the Holy One of Israel and of Jesus Christ. Loving the other, the neighbour, in whatever relationship and with whatever intensity, hurts one into the awesome encounter with the creating-reconciling God. Genuine human loving in friendship as in marriage, in what Pope John Paul II has called a civilisation of love as opposed to a civilisation of hatred and war, involves exposure to God, makes one vulnerable to the holy and to the further creating and reconciling work of the holy, and at serious breakdown to the process of repentance and forgiveness in social as well as personal terms. A world largely at peace with itself will be a world in which friendship prevails between persons and peoples, between races and religions. That kind of friendship is focused on the other person and the other people in creating-reconciling action, the friendship that is vulnerable to the other and so to the holy.

Friendship, sexuality and marriage
Sexuality plays a role in all friendship, in all human relationships. It is embodied sexual beings who encounter one another, are vulnerable to one another. Indeed human sexuality in its spiritual-embodiedness is a key element in the human attraction and gradual bonding characteristic of friendship. For most friendships, this may be a largely sub-conscious element although it may readily come to consciousness in certain circumstances without changing the simple friendship character of the relationship. One has only to attend to the distinctive tone of one's friendships with men and women, if one is lucky enough to have both kinds, to realise how sexuality affects both casual and close friendship. Therein lie once more the gift or promise

and the threat. Unless the creative and reconciling energies of friendship are effectively working, the friends may easily drift apart or more painfully deteriorate in an exploitative shallow sexual intimacy. All developed friendship includes an intimacy of mind and heart, of emotion and body with its own repertoire of expression. Its power lies in the focus on the other and so on its openness to that other and to her or his personal and ultimate mystery, the holy. Without real openness and vulnerability to the human other in herself or himself with all their irreducibility, there cannot be openness to the ultimate other, the divine Holy. To use the human other as a stepping stone to the Ultimate is as much a betrayal as to use the other for one's own immediate satisfaction. In all this the dynamic of sexuality is at work to nourish the friendship or to destabilise and ultimately destroy it. The very contours of the human sexual body, with their spiritual, mental and emotional companions, express both the reaching out to and receiving of the other in the most intimate and inclusive way. When this loving communion is also life-giving in the procreative sense, the love that was friendship now becomes fully sexual and in permanent commitment transcends simple friendship into marriage. In that unique relationship, friendship is transformed but not erased. In the course of a developing marriage the friendship between the spouses must develop also. As with Jesus and his disciples the final goal of marriage and family is fuller friendship – between husband and wife and between parents and children.

Only the experience of marriage itself can capture the highs and lows of its directly sexual expressions. Even the communion in one flesh may be variable in its loving significance and personal completion as it reflects the varying health and happiness of the spouses and of their relationship. In their daily living and loving they encounter, reveal and cherish more of each other's distinctiveness, strangeness and otherness. All this is heightened by their sexual otherness, the desire it kindles and the fear it may provoke in its very strangeness. Poets and painters have attended to the wonder and excitement of newly-weds (or lovers) undressing for the first time. The revealing and concealing in their vulnerability move on delicately to touch and taste, to smell and sound. So through the five senses the couple prepare for the sexual intimacy of one-flesh union, the closest and most profound giving and receiving of the other. In Christian understanding this is no longer a giving and receiving of just the human other. From Adam's brief love-song in Genesis through the Song of Songs and onto the explicit connection between marital love and that of Yahweh/God for his people, invoked by the prophets Hosea and Isaiah, as well as that of Christ for his church, marriage and married loving carry a divine surplus. In expressing their vulnerability to each other so fully and powerfully, the married also express their vulnerability to the holy. As marriage is for Christians a sacrament so the marital act of union is by the same token of sex (nature) and grace, holy-making.

Justice in love

One of the persisting dangers of the recovery of the primacy of love in Christian living, including Christian marriage, and in its theological companion, moral theology, is the ignoring or even suppression of justice as essential to all human and divine-human relationships. St Thomas Aquinas, to whom Professor Lawlor has always acknowledged his indebtedness, has several insights on justice relevant to this meditation. His definition of justice may be summarised as giving the other her due. The otherness of the other so central here demands the kind of respect, recognition and response which the most exalted feeling of love may not ignore, still less suppress. In the more juridical presentation of marriage and of morality generally prior to Vatican II, legal and justice considerations predominated to the extent that marriage's supreme expression of loving in sexual intercourse was described in terms of the *debitum*, what was due simply in justice. Moving beyond that understanding was clearly necessary, but without permitting some sentimental view of love to eliminate the mutual respect due in justice. Of course the justice-in-love requirements of marriage extend far beyond the marital act, central as that is. In financial arrangement as in domestic duties and still more in parenting, justice and its dimensions of due and equality should flourish. Too many marriages and friendships perish through the injustice of one or both parties. Without the hard edge of justice in genuine respect for and sharing with the other, the love, which Aquinas described as the form of all the virtues, collapses into sentimentality, separation and even hatred. Without that formative love justice can easily become the harsh boundary of the separate.

In another teasing insight, Aquinas describes the virtue of religion, by which human beings relate to God, as a subset of justice. Worship is due to God in justice. For Aquinas the Christian theologian, charity was still the primary virtue and the form of the virtue of justice in all its dimensions. He was however echoing the close connection in the scriptures, particularly the Hebrew scriptures, between divine justice and mercy, Yahweh's love and compassion for his people and his characteristic justice. Love of God and love of neighbour, already to the fore in the Hebrew scriptures and given utter primacy by Jesus, incorporate without ambiguity the justice due to God and neighbour. In practicing that justice to the neighbour one is also reaching out to God, vulnerable to the holy. 'As long as you did it to one of these least ones ...' Justice in marriage love, beyond patriarchy or matriarchy, beyond sentimentality, neglect or violence, provides a profound opening to the transcendent as each encounters more fully the holy in the other.

Hurt, healing and the holy
'No love, no marriage' became a kind of slogan in the sixties and seventies even if it did not convince many marriage tribunals at the time. 'No hurt, no love' might sound a more forbidding note. Yet human experience and Christian revelation would seem to endorse it. Not that either would glorify hurt or seek it as some badge of authentic loving. It seems rather the inevitable companion of human existence, including that exalted form of human existence, love. For bodily beings pain and mortality seem inescapable. For embodied spirits the pain turns personal into a mental sense of hurt. In human relations, given that people remain at best half-strangers in the half-light, misunderstandings and worse are to be expected. Intimacy and estrangement are never far apart. The Jewish-Christian history of the intimacy-estrangement dialectic at human and divine-human level hardly needs further rehearsing. And it opens up to a second strand of that history, the creating-reconciling strand. In marriage as in friendship the creating and reconciling dynamic is the source of growth through the shared joys and sometimes divisive hurts. In the shared celebration of the joys and in the mutual forgiveness of the hurts, the sacrament of marriage realises the healing and holy-making presence of the incarnate God.

CHAPTER NINE

Friendship, Marriage and the Risk of God

Friendship has not featured significantly in Christian thinking or its more formal expression, theology, for a very long time. This has been even more true of Christian thinking about marriage. When the pre-Vatican II contractual and juridical language about marriage was largely replaced by the more personal language of love, the love of friendship did not receive any more attention from the theologians of marriage. This may have been partly responsible for the underdevelopment which the 'new' theology of marriage still displays, although this has more basic reasons such as the limited role of married theologians in this area and the crises which marriage itself is experiencing in the traditionally Christian West. Indeed it is likely that all three of these elements, the uncritical attitude to love in theology at the expense of friendship, the limited influence of married theologians and the strains on marriage itself, have converged to weaken the Christian understanding of marriage and, at the official level, pushed it back towards pre-conciliar analysis and attitude.

The return of friendship
In this context the return of friendship as a theological topic may be a sign of hope. Too much should not be made of the return. To vary an old joke, a few swallows in the shape of articles and books do not make a Summa. Recent major dictionaries of theology, a minor growth industry, do not carry substantial or even separate articles on friendship. In the traditionally central theological disciplines of biblical studies and of fundamental and systematic theology, friendship scarcely rates a mention. In the newer disciplines of liturgical studies and ecumenical theology friendship is similarly absent. Only in moral theology, the theology of Christian living, in feminist theology or more accurately much of the theology by women theologians, and in spiritual

94

theology does it feature. For moral theology, friendship is still peripheral although this may still be its most likely point of entry into mainstream theology, especially in the relational mode in which it is being developed by women. Spiritual theology is still unfortunately regarded by many professionals as marginal and derivative. Of course this too is changing and the older established disciplines are finding it increasingly difficult to maintain their distinctiveness and justify their sense of superiority. The return of friendship as a central theological topic will hasten this overdue restructuring.

Christian faith and theology are not the only areas of life and thought suffering from lack of due attention to friendship and experiencing some uncertain signals of its return. In recent decades the field of ethics has provided some of the stronger signals. No doubt ethics had experienced the absence of any discussion of friendship quite sharply, particularly when attention turned once more to Aristotle's ethics and to its treatment of the topic. This development, particularly in the work of people like Alasdair McIntyre, informed some of the moral theologians' renewed interest in friendship mentioned earlier. True to Aristotle's own concerns, McIntyre and others recovered the notion of civic friendship, friendship as a social political possibility and not just a personal one. Indeed in Aristotle and many of his closest followers from Aquinas to McIntyre, friendship has always a social significance and is not confined to the purely personal and often sentimental notion of modern usage.

The social and political dimensions of friendship have important implications in criticising and meeting such continuing threats to personal freedom and social solidarity as tribalism and sectarianism, authoritarianism and individualism as well as the emerging Western-style threats of fragmentation to all persons and their relationships. Further reflection on these signs of the return and need of friendship across a broad spectrum of human structures and practices will be required as the discussion of friendship and its relation to marriage in a Christian context develops.

Others in communion: An analysis of friendship
Friendship is a very ancient concept and practice in a wide range of civilisations. Its meaning and function cannot, however, be simply assumed as obvious and consistent over time and cul-

ture. Aristotle's integration of friendship into his ethics has proved a fertile source of Western thinking on the matter as indicated above. Yet his exclusion of women, children and slaves from equality with male citizens restricted a practice of friendship involving ideas of equality and reciprocity. His requirement of equality also excluded the concept of human friendship with God(s). And his categorising of friendship under the headings of pleasure, use and goodness (virtue), while illuminating, appear too rigid in a culture which values the pleasure and support which the company of friends offers. The Hebrew tradition is typically less interested in analysis than in narrative and the stories of David and Jonathan and of Ruth and Naomi, while culturally remote, offer still relevant accounts of some of the virtues and vicissitudes of friendship. At least implicit in the Hebrew tradition, and quite explicit in its Christian sequel, is the acceptance of human friendship with God providing new challenges to the ideas of equality and reciprocity between friends.

Christianity created its own difficulties for human friendship with its primacy of charity (agape) appearing at times to devalue love between humans in face of the call to love God, and to devalue particular human loves in face of the universal call of charity. The renewed interest in the Irish tradition of the anam chara (soul friend) offers a different perspective on both human friendship and divine-human relations and is proving a further sign of the return of friendship to theological thinking.

Without reaching beyond the Western tradition, it is clear that the understanding and practice of friendship are greatly influenced by social and cultural conditions. They may in that sense be said to be social constructs. This should not be taken in some entirely positivist or arbitrary sense as if an individual or society were simply capable of inventing some entirely new and discontinuous understanding or practice of friendship today. Linguistic and cultural continuities with their biological and other roots are much too strong to be simply shed in that fashion. Yet practices, their analysis and understanding change in friendship as in all human realities.

Among recent developments in philosophy and ethics, as in moral theology, one of the more fruitful for our purposes has been a consideration of human beings in relationship, personal and communal, in terms of human otherness. Human beings as others to one another, as different and discontinuous, indeed strangers, describe a critical initial condition of every human encounter. The encounter of parents and new-born child is the most commonplace if also the most paradoxical example of this. It is also one of the more instructive. This tiny helpless and frequently demanding bundle of their own flesh and blood comes to the parents as fully other as they are, and a total stranger whose character and destiny they will only slowly, sometimes painfully and never more than partially, learn. For the child, parents are other and stranger also although she has difficulty in differentiating, in discovering boundaries of self and of other, even of mother, perhaps particularly of mother.

The otherness involved in all human encounters establishes a relationship, a community, however shallow and fleeting. Indeed human encounter of others is only possible in some already given communal reality. It occurs in a particular social context like the family or the school or the golf club. The social context of the human encounter of others is eventually planet wide as world travellers of today readily attest. More significantly it is humanity wide. A potential human community of others offers the prospect of relationships and friendships between human individuals and groups across all religious, cultural, ethnic and gender boundaries. It is here that the New Testament, with its claim that the boundaries between Jew and Gentile, male and female, bond and free are overcome in Jesus Christ (Gal 3:28), transcends the limits implicit in Aristotle.

This fast forward into theology has not taken full account of the difficulties and possibilities of the otherness approach to friendship. Without the differentiation of human otherness, relationships like friendship would be impossible. Yet the immediate overtone of friend is of similarity rather than difference, while that of otherness is of distance, even opposition rather than closeness. Of course there is no human otherness without some similarity however overlooked, and no human closeness without some distance however disguised.

In the simple one-to-one model of two people, recognition of the other as other, as a unique centre of human being, of human knowing and loving, feeling and acting, as irreducibly other, establishes the basic distance between the others, but only on the presumption of a shared humanity with all the communal elements that implies at biological, psychological, cultural and spiritual levels. (How these different levels are named and interpreted may vary widely.) Recognising the uniquely different as human other implies continuity with that other. It also enables (fuller) recognition of the self as unique other. Other-recognition as it develops and deepens involves developing and deepening self-recognition or self-understanding. Other-recognition becomes possible in the first place, e.g. for the baby, by recognition from others, e.g. the parents.

The call to recognition which the presence of the other, baby or adult, embodies is at the heart of moral relationship in the Western and Christian traditions. It includes a call to respect the other in her otherness and to respond to her in her needs. All this is possible within some accepted commonality, particularised in others as groups as well as individual persons. Focused as appropriate on specific aspects of need and developed over time recognition, respect and response can lead to a truly personal community, to others becoming ever more fully differentiated in deeper communion. This moral life may also be described in the parallel structure of the virtues as the habitual commitments and skills to seek the good of the others and so of the self. The relational and virtue approaches to morality come together in this way and lead into an analysis of friendship in moral terms and of morality in friendship terms.

Three further elements of friendship as the communion of others must be attended to here, even if they cannot by fully developed. The discussion so far has been abstract and general, even universal in its apparent applicability to all human relationships. Friendships are concrete and particular, at least as they are usually conceived or better recounted. Friendship is the stuff of narrative rather than philosophy, of story rather than analysis. The mutual recognition, respect and response, the moral demands of all authentic human relations however fleeting, need time, story-time and story-line to flower in friendship.

The story-line of friendship moves beyond intellectual moralising into the realm of imagination and feeling, of affection and empathy, of sympathy and compassion. Aristotle's vision of friendship as virtue can seem cold and even calculating without the warmth and spontaneity which particular friendships always involve. In the laughter and the tears, in the celebration and the grieving, the bonds of friendship are nourished and refined. Emotional bonding is an integral part of true friendship, providing the compost in which recognition, respect and response can properly flourish, in which virtue becomes rooted. The twists and turns of the story of any friendship reflect the emotional highs and lows of the friends, and depend for survival on their commitments and skills, their mastery of the virtue.

And the story is open-ended. Friendships are always incomplete even at death. In the language of otherness there is always more of each to be discovered and realised. Sometimes the discovery may be unwelcome, even destructive. Friends can part in bitterness and cries of betrayal. Human otherness is at once gift and threat. Human relations carry an ambiguity in which the threat may triumph over the gift. In family or in neighbourhood relations, as in the most intimate friendship, the potential for destruction and division can never be simply overlooked or eliminated. The moral call is to focus on the gift of the other, to develop or restore mutual trust and enrichment. Indeed the development and the restoration usually have to go on simultaneously. Reconciliation, in the New Testament sense of bringing others into unity *(diallassein)*, is part of the permanent task of friendship.

Friendship, justice and liberation
Within both the Aristotelian and Christian traditions justice is based on otherness, human otherness. *Ad alterum*, in relation to the other, is for Aquinas the distinguishing feature of justice. Its practice consists in rendering to the other her due. In discussion of friendship and of marriage justice seldom figures nowadays, overshadowed as it may be by love or affection. This is more clearly true of friendship than of marriage although the dominantly patriarchal model of marriage even in the recent past implied serious injustices to women and children. In friendship, values like justice and truth maybe taken for granted beneath the overt affection and regular companionship. These may also cover deep rivalries and resentments which issue in unjust and deceitful manipulation of one or both friends. Recognition and respect for the otherness of the other, essential to friendship, involve a critical exercise of justice. Without the attitude and practice of justice, friendship becomes fraud.

Justice as giving the other her due (in recognition, respect and response) is letting the other be her (true) self. It sets her free, liberates her. In the reciprocity of friendship the self is in

turn liberated by the other. Mutual liberation and empowerment is characteristic of true friendship. Some qualifications
must be immediately added. The model here is first of all personal friendship, although liberation in current usage generally
refers to the political or social, which will be discussed later.
Secondly, even true friendship is not perfect friendship and
there will usually be some elements of enslavement or exploitation built into the most liberating friendship. Friends will always remain some threat to each other even where they are
genuinely and predominantly gift.

Friendship and its liberating potential take time. First encounters in family, or the larger social setting of school or work-
place or neighbourhood, may or may not flower into friendship.
To get to know and accept one another, friends need shared
time, time shared in conversation and common activities. Over
time the several dimensions of human relations, physical, emotional, mental and spiritual, become involved in a bonding
process which issues in the unity or community of friends.
Others-in-communion share feelings as well as interests, standards as well as activities. They still remain other. Their very irreducibility as others provides the resources for the deeper
bonding which easy or assumed similarity could not reach. Of
course such otherness will at some stage create problems.
Mutual threat will recur but the bonding already in place and
the trust it has generated should enable further liberation and
deeper communion. Disputes and estrangements call on that
deeper human and Christian value of reconciliation, bringing
the others together beyond the pain of estrangement into the renewal of friendship.

The personal model needs still further investigation in terms
of various needs of human difference, of gender and race for example. However, the balance between personal and social is always at risk in these discussions. Remembering the Christian
tradition of Jesus' disciples as a community of friends and the
philosophical political tradition initiated by Aristotle of civic
friendship, attention will now centre on the social dimension of
friendship, in church and society.

Friends, disciples and citizens
Friend and friendship are deeply embodied in Jesus' ministry
and teaching as recorded in the gospels. Disciples are designated

friends. Jesus has a range of particular friends from the beloved disciple to Martha, Mary and Lazarus. His provocative friendships with women was only one aspect of his befriending the social inferiors and outcasts of his time, like his eating and drinking with prostitutes and sinners. His more radical teaching on the love of neighbour as exemplified in the story of the Samaritan on the road to Jericho or in his injunction about love of enemies reached its climax on the Cross. There he finally laid down his life for his friends while praying for his enemies, 'Father forgive them for they know not what they do.'

The disciple-friends of the early Christian community expressed their discipleship in close-knit communities whose central self-identification was eating and drinking together the Body of the Lord. The tensions and the threats occurred also between the leaders of different churches like Peter and Paul, or within local churches themselves such as that of Corinth. And as the members grew and the local churches become more far flung, the friendship-discipleship became more difficult to maintain. Practices of hospitality for visiting disciples and above all the offering of the bread that was the Body of the Lord as the symbol of unity in Christ sustained a sense of community, of bonding and of more deeply rooted friendship. As the basilicas replaced the catacombs and the church became institutionalised along Roman and imperial lines, the strain on the friendship model became ever greater.

At the same time the loving unity became more theological in tone, founded in the love of God for us, enabling us to love God and one another. Love was the touchstone. 'Love and do what you will,' was Augustine's summary. And this love was in danger of becoming more theoretical. The scale, the structure and primacy of love of God could lead disciples, leaders and followers, into overlooking the immediate, concrete and affective love for the person next door.

Ancient social structures in family and society, from patriarchy to slavery, involved unloving personal injustices, endured by wives and children, slaves and strangers. The radical practice and teaching of Jesus in his personal and community relations were as yet unable to breach these inherited structures. Of course there were significant personal relationships in the developing church which could be models of friendship even today. This became more evident as the early moved into the medieval.

But until the medieval theologians, mystics and saints, friendship was a neglected resource for Christian living and church renewal.

Many of the present-day fault-lines in the church reflect the decline of the friend-disciple model. Heavy juridical structures and a contest between (fundamentalist) communalism and (unrestrained) individualism are paralysing Christian community and personal living. The revival of a church based on disciples-friends with their equality and mutuality would help transform the present mutually antagonistic and enslaving groups and individuals. It would also liberate the church to perform its graceful role of sacrament of society, as sign and promoter of the community of humankind.

In Western society in particular, despite the positive developments in regard to equality and freedom through human rights and participatory government, social relations are under threat from an enervating individualism and a shallow secularism. Civic friendship with effective and affective relations between persons and communities is essential to overcoming present rivalries and fragmentations. For civic friendship to develop some deeper and more sacred sense of person is needed than that usually associated with the litigious citizen – subject of rights. The reverence for persons and the bonding of communities, with particular regard for the deprived and marginalised which should characterise the good society, could be best described and achieved in terms of civic friendship.

In all this the community of disciples-friends could once again play its sacramental role. The sacred otherness of the human person and the commitment in solidarity to justice for all could reveal the human reality and its divine depths for now obscured by secular individualism. The rediscovery of the sacred dimension of humanity depends then on the rediscovery of ecclesial and civic friendship.

Eros, philia, agape
The three Greek terms which have dominated exploration of love over the centuries may still be usefully employed in terms of desire-love (including sexual desire), friendship-love, and Christian love. Their origins and history, including their Christian history, are too lengthy and complex to be followed through here. Present usage is in its turn varied and disputable.

The employment and examination of the terms emphasised in this context will hope to remain faithful to the origins and history while being credible and accessible to contemporary readers. *Eros* or desire-love moves the loving subject towards another attracting subject or even object. As distinct from *philia* or *agape* it can focus on objects, beautiful or valuable or at least appealing to the desiring subject. Here the concern is with eros-love as it operates between (personal) subjects. Desire-love may develop into friendship love and even Christian love but unlike them it seeks at first the good of the desirer-lover rather than that of the desired-loved. It is what attracts and hopefully satisfies the desiring subject that is the trigger. In the further exchange of human subjects, desire may begin to fit into a broader context, eros may begin to assume some of the reciprocity and benevolence of philia.

Yet eros remains a powerful force in human life and love and a positive one in many instances. It is the beginning of many fulfilling relationships of friendship and marriage. It witnesses to the fundamentally and properly pleasurable nature of so much of creation as God in the creation myths of Genesis revealed. The delight that crowns eros-love in sexual and other activities has its own revelatory significance.

Eros-love may easily become distorted as the desire suppresses the love. In the desire for power or money, for sexual or more trivial gratifications, love may be totally lost. Philia or friendship-love, with its emphasis on equality, mutuality and the good of the other, provides over time the proper setting for eros-love. The corruptions to which eros is prone may be corrected and transformed by the development of philia. Philia, which could in turn lack warmth and joy as it concentrates on duty, may be enriched by eros, the desire for, the delight in the company of the other.

Agape is in Christian terms love resourced by the God who *is* love, while also finding its final term in that God. It is God's gift of God's love to human beings through Jesus Christ, enabling them to love God and the neighbour after the fashion of Jesus Christ. Jesus Christ is the key, not simply in his divine origin and destiny but in his human history. Agape-love cannot escape or skip over the human. It must move through these supremely human dimensions of eros and philia. It does not replace them. It transforms them. In personal and ecclesial history agape as love of God has been used to suppress human relations with neighbour or spouse or children. The corruptions by which people are used as stepping-stones to God or ignored in the pursuit of loving God only, need the corrections of philia and eros. Human friendship and its delights belong in the broad sweep of agape as creation emerges from God and returns to God.

The equality and mutuality, the dynamism and delight which the Christian vision of the triune God reveals, offers the final model for the integration of eros, philia and agape into human relations and communities. Beyond that, God's own delight in the universe, God's care for it and the promise of its fulfilment and transformation in Hebrew and Christian scriptures, reveals that the ecclesial and human communities of friends are also called to be friends of the earth. The corruptions and corrections will arise here too but the model and ministry of Christ and his Father, the Creator-God will provide the necessary guidance.

Marriage as friendship: Marriage as sacrament
The extended treatment of friendship as against the brief discussion of marriage offered here may be justified on several grounds. Friendship has been the neglected pole in this discussion. The number of theological articles and books published on marriage even since Vatican II far exceeds the number on friendship. Much of the central Catholic theology of marriage has been covered in previous issues of INTAMS review and even in this one. In some senses there is little new to say on the Christian meaning and characteristics of marriage. Although a much more serious dialogue is still necessary between theology of marriage and the immediate experience of married couples as well as with the empirical sciences, theology as dialogue partner might look again at its own resources. Here the friendship-believer model of church must have serious repercussions on the whole range of church relations and nowhere more so than on those of marriage and the family. The very sacramentality of the church, as effective sign of the relations between God and humanity and between Christ and the disciples, of the call and reality of all people to human community, will be more explicitly and effectively demonstrated by a church as community of believer-friends.

Christian marriage of course shares in this sacramentality of the church as the Letter to the Ephesians implied. Aspects of this sacramentality of Christian marriage as vocation and witness are more fully developed by Professor Anne-Marie Pelletier elsewhere. The stress here is on the friendship character of marriage in its sacramental revelation of the reciprocity in affection and delight, in unity and service of the other. Such marriage promotes a revitalisation for family, church and society of the eros, philia and agape which Jesus manifested and which is rooted in the three-in-one God.

Friendship, marriage and the risk of God
Friendship is delightful and demanding. The best of friends fall out, sometimes irremediably. Betrayal of the friend is as old as humanity and as poignant as the Judas story. Friendship is a risky business. So is marriage. Sharing so much of the fragility of human nature and relationships, of the threat as well as the gift of the others, friendship and marriage begin in risk and remain risk-laden through their history. The unknown other, who remains finally unknown in the most intimate relationship, always poses a threat, which like all aspects of human relations is mutual. What will occasion the realisation of the threat nobody can be sure. The only insurance, and it is not absolute, is the gradual deepening of the knowledge and love and care for each other which friendship and marriage involve. Without risk there is of course no life and no love. The model here is once again the God of creation and redemption. The risks involved in creation, and above all in the creation of living and loving beings who could enter into reciprocal relations of friendship with the Creator, were rapidly realised. The breakdown of relations between Creator and creatures, between the human couple so recently hymning their one-flesh relationship, and between humanity and earth entrusted to it, is rightly the subject of heroic myth in the Book of Genesis. The merging of myth and history in the Hebrew scriptures manifests more fully the risks and indeed the failures of God. The risk deepens with the last throw, sending God's own Son. They would surely honour him.

Calvary tells another story. The breakthrough of resurrection did not see the end of divine risk-taking frustrated by human failure. The history of the church has so many instances to recount. Yet the divine initiatives have had their successes too, not least in the commitments of Christian friends and spouses. So new generations may take heart as the risen Lord is with them in their own risky ventures of loving and life-giving. The risks taken by God provide encouragement and enablement for men and women in their own risk-taking.

That risk-taking in friendship and marriage in committed response to the human other has a deeper dynamic. In a more secular culture, when the absence rather than the presence of God is the more marked, the human other in her attractiveness, in her capacity for equal and mutual relationship, in her courage to enter into marriage-union, offers also an inexhaustible source of loving and being loved. Eros and philia can provide the gateway to agape. Human otherness in friendship and marriage can open the path to divine otherness. Friendship and marriage draw people beyond themselves. They suggest a transcendence of the human partnership. They encourage the risk of following through to the inexhaustible and finally unknowable origin and fulfilment of such living and loving, the ultimate in otherness. They move people towards the great risk of God, of accepting and delighting in the God who is love.

CHAPTER TEN

Homosexuality:
Sorrowful Mystery, Joyful Mystery

A straight view and its origins

The recent painful controversies surrounding Christian attitudes to homosexuals, or 'gay men and lesbians' as they prefer
to be called, have been a source of deep sorrow to many committed Christians, straight and gay. From Reading, Oxford and
Canterbury to New Hampshire, Massachusetts and Washington
DC, on to the centre of old-world Christianity at Rome and beyond, to centres of new-world Christianity like Nigeria, a great
deal of animosity and sometimes hatred on both sides has been
voiced in words and tones unworthy of disciples of the God
who is love.

Taking some imaginary high moral ground, however, above
the abusing parties, simply reveals one's own blind-sight. No
human is above the messy ground of sexual controversy.
Historical hurts, vested interests and hidden agendas, hidden
even from protagonists themselves, abound. Yet it should not be
impossible for Christians, summoned before all to love one another while doing the truth in that love, to conduct an enriching
rather than impoverishing debate, to bear with the pain of, for
the present perhaps, irreconcilably different understandings,
but within a reconciling and reconciled community, as St Paul
put it.

THE SORROWFUL MYSTERY

Religious, cultural and educational background

Any one lifetime offers much too short a period and much too
narrow an experience on which to base an adequate analysis of
an issue as ancient and as complex as homosexuality. These reflections will not attempt such analysis. Yet in the seventy plus
years of life there may be enough experience of friendship and
working with gay people, of pastoral care and academic study,
for the author to presume he may have something helpful to say.

Like most Irish (and other) people who grew up in the thirties and forties, discussion of sex with parents or teachers never occurred. At primary school level and in a farming community, a certain amount of schoolboy chat, including the famous schoolboy smutty stories, provoked a certain response but provided largely misinformation as emerged later. And it's pretty certain that the word homosexuality never surfaced. At secondary school, which was boarding, formal sexual education was nil although there were occasional opaque talks on 'growing up' and the occasional pamphlet available. In that turbulent adolescent period there was plenty of conversation among the students and probably a fair amount of practice, mainly masturbation but also some actual homosexual activity between older and younger boys. However, the conversation was mainly about girls, certainly among the older boys and focused on either the sisters of fellow-students or on the girls in the neighbouring convent schools. Students would also comment on some of the priest teachers having favourite students but it did not seem, according to the grapevine, ever to get beyond the harmless.

By Leaving Cert, and for some well before, students had acquired a basic understanding and vocabulary sufficient, it was thought, to deal with the grand and threatening sexual world outside. How they actually dealt with it, who can say? In memory students who were regarded as highly sexed and were reputed to be sexually active in school turned out to be fairly straight heterosexuals going on to marriage and family. At that stage such gay crushes and the sometimes accompanying activity belonged most likely to what came to be called developmental homosexuality. How many of these who were active ever became adult homosexuals as unmarried or even after marriage there is no way of knowing.

For those who entered the seminary after school in the hope of ordination to the priesthood, there was a course in human biology which was biologically comprehensive but personally and relationally empty. Some further affective education was supplied by talks from Spiritual Directors and Deans, as they were then called, but without particular personal direction either. This was the late forties and early fifties and through fear or embarrassment the buck was always being passed from one set of mentors to another and back to the parents 'who should have done all this years before'. As if any of these groups could give to others what they had never received themselves.

Within the formal walls of theology a little more help was forthcoming. Although the text books provided (in Latin) were appallingly narrow, there was at least one really humane teacher in the Maynooth Moral Theology Department which dealt with sexuality. Canon (later Monsignor) John McCarthy, a priest of Elphin Diocese and subsequently Parish Priest of Athlone, had a personal and pastoral touch which put the students much more at ease with themselves sexually. Jack, as he was called, was no liberal. He taught the rather narrow orthodoxy of his time but allowed for the needs of people and priests in sexual as in other areas. There was no question of relaxing the regular restrictions on homosexuality but there was little emphasis on it and the humane background of the teacher helped some students to treat homosexuals more thoughtfully later.

In the intervening period from ordination in 1955 to first teaching at Maynooth in 1960, moral theology with other sections of Catholic theology had been undergoing a revolution. All this did not start in the 1950s but the publication of two major works in that period, the Redemptorist Bernhard Häring's *The Law of Christ* and the Jesuit Gerard Gilleman's *The Primacy of Charity in Moral Theology*, by title and content gave a whole new direction to Catholic moral theology, including the theology of sex and marriage. In 1962, Häring accompanied by his Irish confrère, Seán O'Riordan, demonstrated the reach of this revolution at the Maynooth Union Summer School on *The Meaning of Christian Marriage*. The setback which this developing theology of sexuality suffered with the publication of *Humanae Vitae* in 1968 did not prevent further exploration into the meaning and purpose of human sexuality in Christian perspective. Homosexuality inevitably figured within this theological exploration, which also realised that it had to continue the dialogue with the world opened up at Vatican II, with the developing human sciences and in the changing moral-cultural context.

Personal and pastoral experience
Late in that traumatic political, cultural and theological year, 1968, a couple of Legion of Mary volunteers found themselves helping a number of young gay men they encountered around O'Connell Street public lavatories. In need of pastoral and theological help, they were referred to the author as a moral theologian. He was forced to admit his ignorance of the pastoral dimensions

of the problem while acknowledging his willingness to help and above all his need to learn. Over a number of years he attended the regular meetings of people who had suffered so much over the years from hidden and isolated lives, sometimes punctuated by verbal and physical abuse despite their discretion. A couple of high points from these years. A day's retreat at the Redemptorist Retreat House at Marianella where the group had found a permanent home after their earlier welcome at the CIE building off O'Connell Street. For the shy and fearful people who made their way from Limerick or Mayo, as well as for the more regular Dublin participants, the genial presence of Auxiliary Bishop Jim Kavanagh as chief celebrant at the afternoon Mass was a real comfort.

About that time the Gay Movement in Dublin decided to hold their first public conference. As no hotel was willing to accommodate them (the Travellers of that time!) the conference was held in Trinity College. Very properly, the group originally organised by members of the Legion of Mary and still faithful to that group and their church, felt that their church should be represented pastorally and theologically at the conference. In the ensuing publicity, some, but only some, of it sensational as might be expected at a first outing of this kind, the author received a good deal of criticism. Indeed if it had not been for the intervention of the then Cardinal, William Conway, he might well have lost his job. He certainly lost his regular invitations to speak in Irish dioceses, while remaining ironically *in situ* in training future Irish clergy.

This was all very trivial in comparison to the prejudice and discrimination which gay people were still enduring. A possibly faulty memory recalls how Declan Costello as Attorney-General had assurances that gay people would not be harassed by the gardaí. In those years also a pastorally courageous but theologically careful pamphlet by Redemptorist moral theologian, Raphael Gallagher, was withdrawn from sale at Veritas Bookshop at the behest of the then Archbishop of Dublin. Many priests and theologians like Raphael Gallagher were providing pastoral care and support. Yet the Catholic Church authorities in Rome and in Ireland remained paralysed by the bio-morality which had condemned homosexuals for so long. Meantime Irish and European society were moving on. The David Norris case against homosexual discrimination, which eventually prevailed in Strasbourg, led to a belated replacement of the Offences against the Person Act of 1861, which had outlawed all homosexual activity, by the relatively liberal act of 1993 introduced by Minister for Justice Máire Geoghegan Quinn. Interestingly this provoked no serious outcry from conservative elements in church or society.

That might look like a happy ending as far as Irish society was concerned, a sorrowful and penal period yielding to a free and joyful one. It was indeed a notable legal advance for gay people. However, laws of themselves do not make for a tolerant and inclusive society as the current language has it. Prejudices and bigotry in this, as in race and religion, do not disappear overnight. Past hurts reach deep and are compounded by real and sometimes imagined present ones. All human beings carry their deep hurts and sorrows for a long time, sometimes even to the grave. Gays and lesbians are no exception to this rule and their oft-times ignorant offenders were in need of healing also from the distortions and hurts of years of anti-gay prejudice and behaviour. The sorrow lingers on.

The impact of HIV/AIDS
In the 1980s a new dimension of suffering and privation, physical, mental and social, hit the gay community with the development of HIV/AIDS, regarded for some time as the gay disease as it was first diagnosed among the gay community in the US. To all its horrendous physical and mental suffering were added further social stigma and isolation. Just recently at an anti-gay rally in the US a placard pictured in *The Guardian* newspaper read 'Let Aids be their Lot' or so. In the 80s a common interpretation among fundamentalist, and some not so fundamentalist, religious groups saw AIDS as divine punishment for homosexual behaviour. Although this era has by and large passed because HIV/AIDS has turned out to be mainly a disease of heterosexuals in the wider world, there are evidently people who still believe in the curse-of-God theory. Such beliefs will usually only surface when a critical issue emerges such as the threat of legalising civil unions for gay people.

A double involvement with the HIV/AIDS pandemic since 1990 has led to increased exposure to the painful realities of homosexual living, suffering and dying. Although no longer a condition exclusive to gay men as noted, a great many gay men have been, and a number are still being, infected. As the ethical-theological member of the Caritas Internationalis Task Force on HIV / AIDS, the writer had to wrestle with all the moral dimensions of the pandemic, including those of homosexuality. Fieldwork in this capacity was mainly in developing countries in Africa and Asia where those infected by the virus are usually but not always heterosexuals, and where gay people with or without the infection may have their existence denied or are otherwise oppressed.

The more direct pastoral experience arose in the early 90s in a parish in Greenwich Village in New York where a lot of young gay men were suffering and dying from AIDS. The contacts have continued on my return visits through a Gay Discussion Group which meets every Sunday in the Rectory. Some rather simple points emerged from these meetings and other pastoral contacts: 1) the ordinariness and diversity of these self-declared gay men (very few lesbians have attended the meetings despite advertising in the Parish Newsletter and other invitations); 2) their commitment to the Catholic faith and church; 3) the suffering endured in a relatively uncomplaining way over the years; 4) their resilience in the face of this; 5) above all, the devotion of one partner confronted with the developing and terminal stages of AIDS in the other. Of course there were rows and crises but in so many instances the love displayed and enacted could only be described in Christian terms as agape-love of neighbour. In that context the pastor and theologian could only marvel at the holy-making love of these men. For him it was a genuinely liberating experience which no heavy-handed teaching by church or other authority could ever obliterate.

The liberation of course was due to the redemptive suffering of the AIDS sufferers and their partners, their sorrowful mystery which the theologian was allowed in some small measure to share. It opened him up more deeply to the mysteries of suffering and death which everybody has to face and with which Christians seek to cope through faith in the redemptive force of the suffering, death and resurrection of Jesus Christ. Even more significantly it confronted the theologian with the mysteries of human loving, friendship and sexuality, particularly the great mystery of human sexual loving in its homosexual as well as its heterosexual forms. For all the joy he had observed and experienced in so many relationships, here he encountered, he

thought, the truly sorrowful mystery of human and sexual loving. Set against this mystery, the codes of the scribes seemed
utterly inadequate. Unfortunately, too many of the Catholic
Church's official statements over these decades seem to concentrate on old codes and lack any sense of the sorrow or the mystery. Pastoral care was never simply lacking. And the practical
responses of so many church organisations and personnel
around the world to people living with HIV/AIDS was often
outstanding. Although the leaders and agents of these remarkable achievements have sometimes been gay or lesbian, church
authorities have at best ignored this and at worst ...

More in sorrow
The offensive language of the recent 2003 document by the
Congregation for the Defence of the Faith may not be excused on
the grounds that it was simply repeating recent teaching by the
same Congregation, without, it may be said, having learned
very much new about courtesy or homosexuality in the meantime. Of course discourtesy and offensive language is never the
prerogative of one side in a heated dispute. Referring to
Cardinal Ratzinger, head of the Congregation, in terms of the
Hitler Youth on a *Morning Ireland* programme did not help the
reasonable and loving debate needed. More disturbing from the
Congregation was its unwillingness or inability to distinguish
between the legal protection of stable gay relationships and
marriage as understood by most Christians and most civil juris-
dictions. The conceit that such a document could impose on
Catholic politicians, operating in today's democratic societies,
the duty to oppose such legal protection seems not only contrary
to the role of the church in society envisaged at Vatican II but utterly futile. The sorrowful mystery of homosexuality will not
disappear quickly, but must certain leaders in a church committed to compassion and redemption in face of the sorrow and the
mystery, continue to exacerbate the sorrow and obscure the
mystery, even for their own loyal members, heterosexual as well
as homosexual?

THE JOYFUL MYSTERY

One of the great strengths of the Catholic-Christian tradition has
been its constant return to the goodness and centrality of the
human bodily condition. Whatever the temptations of Manicheism,

Puritanism and Jansenism in their recurring religious or secular forms, the doctrines of creation and incarnation with their sacramental expressions have enabled the church to rediscover its bodily balance through the millennia. One of the truly exciting times of rediscovery in sex and marriage, the most perilous aspects of bodily existence, was that of the Second Vatican Council. The joy, embodied joy, was back. *The Pastoral Constitution on the Church in the Modern World* was the Council's most effective response to the prophets of doom against whom Pope John XXIII had warned in his opening speech to the Council.

The very first words of the constitution, the Latin *Gaudium et Spes*, by which such documents are generally known, proclaimed loud and clear the primary message of joy and hope which the Council was offering church and world. (And the sorrows and struggles were not overlooked.) In its treatment of sex and marriage, as in other matters, the joy and hope transformed the rather legal and negative earlier account into a vision of marriage as a community of love and life. Sexual attraction, sexual love, sexual union and sexual life-giving were presented more in the biblical spirit of the Song of Songs than in the juridical spirit of the Code of Canon Law, the presiding source for the church's approach to marriage in previous decades.

The context of the goodness of sex and marriage as part of God's gift in creation, and their reaffirmation in incarnation, was clearly set forth. And the spirit of embodied, loving joy, which was originally confirmed by the Pentecostal sending of the Holy Spirit, could confidently embrace human sexuality and the fullness of its realisation in marriage. Despite the negative vibes generated a short time later by *Humanae Vitae*, with its insistence that each individual act of intercourse be open to life-giving, the basic thrust of its understanding of the joyful relationship between love and life in sexual communion remained faithful to Vatican II.

A great deal remained and remains to be done in exploring the mystery of human sexuality in its powerfully creative and destructive modes. Some of this exploring may be more insightfully pursued by artists rather than philosophers, theologians or various associated scientists. Very often the sense of the mystery is better preserved in the great love stories in novel, film or drama while the great love poems and love songs communicate so much of the mystery and its related worship. That so many of these are secular in form and content should not faze the reader of the Song of Songs or the practitioners of the church's sacramental worship. The God who created all things is the source of all human creativity, artistic as well as religious, sexual as well as intellectual. And the God who became human also became sexual. For all his celibacy, as it might be termed, Jesus was a sexually loving being, as his close friends, men and women, might testify.

Mystery and morality
The mystery of sex and the power and awe which it can awaken do not automatically lead to the joyful. The awe may readily turn to dread, leading to anguish and repression rather than joy. Such distortions have at times afflicted most religions and societies. There are persistent streaks of such paralysing fear not only in most cultures but in many individuals in every culture, with overtones of immaturity and unease. More evident in the Western world at this time is the opposite failure, the near worship of sex and uninhibited sexual activity by so many. Curiously this may not be a positive cherishing of the human body at all, as Louvain theologian Roger Burgraeve among others, has pointed out. Where bodies, one's own and others', have become mere instruments of pleasure without any serious personal and spiritual involvement, the split between spirit and body has resurfaced. A new dualism violates that human, Christian-Catholic understanding of the embodied spirit and inspirited body so deeply rooted in human experience and Christian revelation. The mystery has been thoroughly cheapened if not entirely lost.

At its best, the tradition of Catholic morality has helped people to recognise and seek to avoid these dualistic distortions of refusing the joyful mystery of human sexuality as fearful and dirty or of splitting sexuality off in its true mystery from the human spirit as some thing to be played with at one's whim, if not substituted for the worship of the one true God in secular game or pseudo-religious rite.

Coming to terms with the mystery of one's sexuality is a life and love task. Only over time and in some continuous love-life will the mystery gradually and partially reveal itself.

Revealing always involves relating and interpreting. In relating to others, human, divine and even cosmic, people begin to discover themselves as different and similar, through the language and skills of interpretation which they learn and then develop in community. So one discovers oneself as a boy, an Irish boy, of a particular family through relational existence and education. One's sexuality develops and is discovered/interpreted in relationship to the same and the different in an interpretative community. Appreciation of its power, its capacity for joy and sorrow, its unpredictability and fierce commitment, all this emerges in the history of relationships, childish, adolescent, adult and elderly. The final mystery eludes but potential for fuller living and deeper relationship persists.

In the course of any one person's history, sexual understanding and behaviour change but always in relationship to some others (even for the monk) and always in a community that is itself changing. Such changes in personal and communal understanding and behaviour have been constant over the past seven decades. Not all for the good of course but not all for the bad either. Reading sexuality in the context of loving creative relationships with its critical expression in marriage as community of love and life, and for Christians as sacrament, offers serious Christians significant guidance that still reflects powerful human and Christian traditions in safeguarding the mystery. It does not however exhaust the possibilities of genuine and faithful sexual loving for Christians and others. In particular, changes in the understanding and practice of homosexual relationships, as witnessed by many dedicated Christians, suggest a more sophisticated analysis of how human embodiment may be expressed lovingly and sexually between same-sex partners with no less stringent demands of course of fidelity and permanence than applies to heterosexual partners. In such situations it would be a mistake to use the term *marriage*, given its hallowed use in all traditions to describe that primary relationship of man and woman with its procreative potential. But it would in certain circumstances be appropriate to offer legal protection to the couple in a whole range of issues, ensuring to some extent their freedom from discrimination and their justice in dealing with one another.

Such acknowledgment in law and charity could liberate many gay couples to contribute more freely and fully to the common good of church and society. It would allow their joy in one another to spill over into the wider community. By revealing the mystery of human sexuality in another form, it could play a redemptive, healing role in a society which in many ways is sexually sick. The joyful mystery would help displace shallow hedonism so prevalent today. What gay people have contributed historically to the arts and to every other dimension of human living could be seen to enhance the most profound of all life's tasks, loving human relationships.

It may seem odd in a reflection of this kind and extent to bypass the usual and usually angry arguments about biblical and church teaching, about biological design and procreative purposes. They have been rehearsed so often and so vigorously that it hardly seemed necessary. Besides, for all their importance in certain contexts and the author's own frequent wrestling with them, they were not to the point in this essay; a semi-autobiographical account of one straight man's journey in seeking at once to cherish, and at least partially to understand, something of the mystery of human sexuality through his encounters with the sorrows and joys of gay friends, acquaintances and clients, if such distinctions really matter.

CHAPTER ELEVEN

Stigmatisation:
HIV-AIDS and Christian Morality

In the course of some thirteen years' work with the Caritas Internationalis Task Force on HIV-AIDS (1990-2003), concentrating but not exclusively on 'developing' countries, the dynamics of the pandemic, as it came to be called, shifted not only from continent to continent but from country to country and indeed from year to year. For the non-medically trained and the non-statistically minded, the regular updates on rates of infection, modes of infection, death rates, drugs developed, their impact, complexity, cost and availability were dizzy-making. Yet the concerned and engaged theologian had to try to keep up if the real theological and moral issues were to be uncovered and offered some, however inadequate, response.

A brief summary of what was always a painful struggle for this and other activist-theologians would cover the recurring and never finally resolved problem of suffering and evil in the world of a good and loving Creator-God. Without continually addressing this problem and in this particular form, a theologian could easily miss the deeper tragedy of the pandemic and the deeper needs of those infected and affected. In addition he could compound their suffering by appearing to support the view that HIV-AIDS was God's punishment for sin. And the sin of course was sexual or otherwise that of the immoral use of drugs. So it was easy to categorise and further marginalise homosexuals, among the first cases to be diagnosed and so named 'the Gay Disease'. As it soon became clear that the disease was not confined to gay men, but that the virus was transmitted by body fluids including sexual fluids, irresponsible sexual behaviour, and its appropriate divine punishment and human stigmatisation, seemed sufficient explanation to the theologically primitive. They had much the same reaction to the infection of drug addicts as exchanging needles meant the sharing of contaminated blood. (Less attention has been paid to those infected by contaminated blood transfusions, to the lack of the technology and the skills to provide 'clean' blood or to the culpability of the suppliers of defective blood.) As the disease spread throughout the world whole peoples, countries and even subcontinents such as sub-Saharan Africa, seemed to fall under divine punishment and human stigmatisation.

Such attitudes, still around if in diminishing degrees, have ignored diverse contexts and deeper influences and so restricted action in prevention, care and therapy. As frequently reported, the spread of HIV and AIDS are intimately related to poverty and its consequences, in lack of health care, education, employment and of the various kinds of personal and social empowerment enjoyed by men and women in wealthier societies. In any overall assessment of the global situation of HIV and AIDS, justice would appear to be the primary virtue despite the valid calls of truth and chastity. And in this connection it seems that much of the argument about the use of condoms as a preventive aid is misleading. Condoms, by the most reliable accounts from the World Health Organisation, UNAIDS and others, can help but they are no panacea for multiple reasons, personal, cultural and industrial. On the other side of the argument, their use should not be simply excluded on religio-moral grounds, certainly not on the grounds proposed by some Catholic Church leaders, adapting as they do the teaching of the encyclical *Humanae Vitae*. Even if that encyclical is taken in its strictest sense, and many Catholics and theologians do not take it in that sense, its ban on contraceptive practices as prevention of the transmission of potential life cannot be applied to the use of condoms to prevent the transmission of potential death. However, all these questions have been adequately rehearsed elsewhere by the present author among others. Some of them will undoubtedly return in developing the major theme of this chapter, the stigmatisation associated with HIV and AIDS and the church's response to that.

The Namibian challenge and the short response
As this material was first presented as the theological paper at a UNAIDS Workshop on Stigmatisation, AIDS and the Christian Churches in Windhoek, Namibia (December 6-12, 2003), it helps to set it in the wider context of the other papers at that work-

shop. Three are particularly relevant in giving the human and ecclesial background and came before this paper which was intended as a theological reflection on or response to them.

In a truly moving personal witness an Anglican priest related his journey from his first awareness of his infection to personal acceptance, to coming out to family and a few friends, to informing his bishop, to his struggles with sickness and medication, to his final discovery of his vocation to peer support for other priests and people infected and affected by the virus. He was echoed at various times in the early stages of workshop by the testimony of young people from Namibia on their experience of being HIV positive.

In his paper, the well-known priest activist and expert on the church's response to HIV and AIDS, Father Bob Vitillo, gave an account of his own experiences of the global church, in its positive and negative responses to the stigmatisation associated with the pandemic. Depressing in his stories of episcopal and clerical rejection and stigmatising, he also had encouraging accounts of positive and caring responses. And he quoted strong messages from the Pope and other Catholic leaders on the Christian obligation to fight stigmatisation and discrimination in the face of HIV and AIDS.

The third paper by one of the joint organisers, theologian and consultant, Gillian Patterson, offered a rich conceptual analysis of stigmatisation, ranging over various perspectives such as the medical, the relation beween stigmatisation and power and some key authors such as Erving Goffmann and Mary Douglas. She also drew an interesting analogy between stigmatisation and sectarianism in Northern Ireland as reported and analysed in the fine publication by Joe Liechty and Cecelia Clegg, *Moving Beyond Sectarianism*.

Clearly it was not possible to absorb, reflect on and respond to such a rich and diverse day by the following morning. The attempt a couple of months later to write up the response, greatly helped by Bob Vitillo's detailed notes, has both the advantages and disadvantages of distance with more time to reflect and more time to forget. However, the wound of exposure to those living with HIV and AIDS and to their supporters and carers, reopened so sharply in Namibia, demands a reconstruction of the response so painfully elicited on that occasion.

In attempting a theological response to the painful issues of stigmatisation and HIV and AIDS from a Christian perspective, it might be well to begin with the short, simple and what at this stage might be termed a religio-moral version. Each human person is created equally in the image of the God of Jesus Christ, is loved equally and unconditionally by that God, not just as an individual but as part of a developing single human community, the one family of God which is destined for the final reign or kingdom of God. That human equality and divine lovableness have been confirmed, renewed and transformed in the incarnation – in the life, death and resurrection of Jesus Christ. Disciples of Christ are called to ensure that each person is treated as a member of divine family and not subjected to stigmatisation, discrimination, exploitation or exclusion, either directly by individuals or indirectly by social structures and processes.

At that level of reflection and teaching it seems clear that the stigmatisation in association with HIV and AIDS is clearly anti-Christian and could and should be countered by Christians taking their faith seriously. Inevitably the solution is not that simple. For one thing Christians are not only, in that hallowed phrase, a communion of saints but also and more obviously a communion of sinners. They are not only graced in person and structure, but also sinful, not only (sometimes) repentant and forgiven but also (sometimes) resistant and relapsing. At some theological gatherings the word sin may be itself stigmatised and excluded, at others it may be exaggerated and exploited. HIV and AIDS are themes that could provoke either extreme.

Creation as differentiation: promise and threat
In the Jewish and Christian vision of the divine creation of the world and humanity, as described particularly in the first chapters of the Book of Genesis, the emergence of the world as a series of differentiations between Creator and creation and within creation itself over the 'six days' is first of all a matter of celebration. At the end of each day's work 'God saw that it was good'. With the creation of human beings as male and female in the very image of God on the sixth day, creation and celebration reached their climax as 'God saw that it was very good'. And creation celebrated itself in the first man's lyrical praise of his partner, as both enjoyed the richness of their created environment in their garden of delight. On this premise and promise God relaxed and rested.

The differentiation of creation soon showed itself as much threat as promise, as chapter three of Genesis illustrates in the story of the fall. Love idyll between man and woman changed to a shame-and-blame game. They saw that they were naked and were ashamed and sewed fig leaves together. At the sound of God in the garden they hid themselves, pretending to God it was because they were naked. In answer to the charge of disobedience the love-lyricist Adam shifted the blame: 'All her fault.' The loving differentiation of creation with all its glorious promise had become estrangement and alienation between creator and creation and within creation, and not only between human beings themselves but between humanity and the rest of creation, as they were banished from the garden of delight and faced the struggle to survive from the earth's fruits and the pain of carrying out that original promise of filling the earth with their progeny and acting as its stewards. The immediate progeny carried the estrangement to fratricide as Cain killed Abel and was condemned to wander the earth. All was not lost, and the divine promise of reconciliation was already at work for humanity and the rest of creation. Even God's special mark on Cain which has often been treated subsequently as punitive stigma, was to protect him from being killed in his turn as a murderer. (Gen 4:15)

The Genesis story is clearly not intended as a historical narrative but as a poetic attempt to understand the complexity in good and evil of the real relationship between a loving and good creator and what must be a fundamentally good creation in the context of human freedom, the threat of estrangement or alienation, the rejection or exclusion of some others as hostile or inferior and so to be stigmatised, to be marked as slaves were marked in the ancient world. In the fuller creation story then the differentiation destined for celebration in communion (Gen 2) lapses into destruction and lamentation but not despair, as the reconciling promise and power of the creator is also at work. (Gen 3 and 4)

This reconciling power and promise is another aspect of the divine other or 'holy one'. In Hebrew the word *qadosh* or other, as applied to God, is translated as 'holy'. That holiness or otherness reveals Yahweh as simultaneously creator and reconciler in divine judgement and mercy. Without the differentiation or otherness from the Creator there is no distinctive creation. With differentiation there is the continuing threat of estrangement calling into action the reconciling power of the Creator. That estrangement affects human-to-human relations, personally and socially, and is rooted in human-to-divine relations. It is that human to human estrangement that results in the various forms of exclusion, hostility, exploitation, violence and stigmatisation. It is that estrangement as sin which the reconciling Creator is continually seeking to overcome through human repentance and divine mercy.

It is possible and helpful to read the Hebrew and Christian scriptures as stories of creation and celebration shadowed by estrangement and destruction to be overcome by repentance and reconciliation. The word 'stranger' constitutes a temptation to rejection in the prophets and an opportunity for hospitality as in the story of Abraham. And stranger as excluded or discriminated against and stigmatised applies to a wide range of peoples and classes and in particular to women, which makes the story of Jesus' encounter with the Samaritan woman one of the significant breaches in both the religious and gender traditions of exclusion and stigmatisation.

A related and relevant scriptural issue in the creation / destruction and recognition / stigmatisation ambiguity is that of sexual differentiation. We have seen how the first sexual love-relationship of Genesis turned to shame and blame. Despite the original created blessing of human sexuality and its wonderful hymn in the Song of Songs by male and female lovers, the Hebrew scriptures contain a great deal of ambiguity, particularly in regard to female sexuality, as references to impurity associated with menstruation and double standards on infidelity illustrate. The New Testament, and particularly the gospels, are free from much of this ambiguity although there are traces of the older tradition in the Pauline writings.

Differentiation and incarnation
In incarnation new and complex forms of differentiation emerge both within God's self and between God and creation in humanity and cosmos. As the 'beloved Son' of the baptism and transfiguration stories becomes the despised, rejected and near-despairing figure on the cross ('My God, My God, why have you rejected me?'), the differentiation within God takes on the shape of profound estrangement akin to that of sinful human estrangement from God. Jesus has, in Paul's words, become sin for us.

And the marks of that sin and its overcoming are his wounds on the cross, the *stigmata* of later Christian tradition. The passion of Christ, for all its theological and dramatic centrality, is not the beginning and end of the Jesus story. The nativity accounts in Matthew and Luke, whatever their historical basis, indicate already the homelessness of God's Son in God's world with no room at the inn and a flight into exile to escape Herod's massacre. The massacre anticipated Jesus' own recognition of his divisiveness, 'bringing not peace but the sword'. The divisiveness reached into his own family in Luke's story of his ignoring his parents and staying behind in the Temple, as well as his later reaction to reports of his family seeking him, 'Who are my brothers and sisters?'

For all the differentiation, otherness and estrangement which the life, ministry and death of Jesus Christ involved, and every page of the gospels reveals a new aspect, his overall mission and its method carried a quite different message, a good-news message of reconciliation and communion between God, humanity and the world ('God was in Christ reconciling the world with Godself') and between human beings. His method carried through his original sending or going like the prodigal son into a far country and seeking the companionship of sinners, the excluded and the stigmatised. His mission would start by establishing table-fellowship and community with the excluded and stigmatised, the sick (including the lepers and 'possessed') and the hungry, the widowed and the bereaved, the prostitutes and tax-collectors and notoriously in his friendship with women, even those menstruating, taken in adultery and belonging to the despised people of Samaria. Jesus was announcing and taking this opportune time *(kairos)* to lay the ground-plan for his disciples in designing a new human community *(kaine koinonia)*, a new creation *(kaine ktisis)* in which there would no longer be any hostile division (discrimination, stigmatisation) between Jew and Gentile (race and religion), male and female (gender), slave and free (class and wealth), but all would be one community with their created and creative diversity in Christ – Paul's vision of the in-breaking reign of God.

To accomplish this, Jesus had to go through the horrors of Gethsemene, of the courts of Caiaphas and Pilate, of the *via dolorosa* to Calvary and to the crucifixion between two thieves. Such a story has its problems. It could and does lead some

Christians to believe that suffering and associated stigmatisation, as in HIV and AIDS, should make those infected and affected simply resigned to their suffering while the rest make
soothing noises from their armchairs. Nietzsche picked up a
continuing temptation of Christians when he described their religion as one of weakness and of victims in which the victims are
to be resigned to their fate as victims. Not unlike Marx's opium
of the people.

But this is really the opposite of what Jesus was about in taking on extreme human suffering. He was not endorsing it or its
agents but, in identifying with the victims and the stigmatised,
he was seeking to overcome suffering and calling on his disciples
to share the sufferings of the others in attempts to understand
and overcome such suffering. Such attempts demand action to
alleviate and prevent, to remove stigmatisation and oppression
by person or structure, to liberate all those whom he identified
in opening his mission in Nazereth as he opened the Book of
Isaiah. (Lk 4) Breaking the silence on stigmatisation would be a
first call on all disciples in a time of AIDS. Conversion of mind
and structure to include fully these so stigmatised would be the
appropriate embodiment of that breach of silence, the incarnation of that human word.

The gifts of the Spirit

The overcoming of estrangement, suffering and death by the
suffering Christ were realised in principle for all in resurrection
and the sending of the Spirit. The further differentiation within
God which this trinitarian pattern revealed provides the ultimate basis for human and cosmic diversity in unity, free of all
oppression or subordination. However, realisation of real diversity in authentic unity within the historical human community
remains partial and damaged, awaiting the fullness of the kingdom. The community of disciples, the church of Christ, receiver
of the Spirit and empowered by holiness of that Spirit, is still a
church bearing the marks of estrangement internally and exter-
nally. It remains a community always in need of forgiveness and
reconciliation while called to be an ambassador of reconciliation
for the whole of God's world. With that call and the accompanying power of the Spirit, the church bears a special responsibility
to confront stigmatisation and its underlying oppressions in the
AIDS crisis.

The power of the Spirit is not akin to that of the human power exercised by emperors and kings. Jesus' kingdom was not of this world like that of Pilate or Caesar. Indeed the whole story of creation and salvation or reconciliation might be read as a story of God's gradual divestment of what would be regarded in human terms as divine sovereignty. In creating, God establishes a cosmic reality and human freedom which God continues to respect. As the story develops, God's inexhaustible and creative loving is challenged by the wayward and hostile otherness of creatures. The final solution, in the incarnation, death and resurrection of Jesus, witnesses the final divine divestment of the conventional power of Lordship which might be experienced as oppressive power. It is only in following Jesus in such divesting that the disciples and their leaders can carry through the process of reconciliation. Only by joining openly with the stigmatised can they hope to bring Jesus' healing and reconciling grace to them. The association of stigma and worldly power mentioned earlier demands of disciples that they follow that self-emptying (kenosis) which Paul hymns in Philippians 2 when the Son no longer thought of himself as equal to God but took the form of a slave (one of the originally stigmatised). For disciples in a time of AIDS it is a hard saying but an evangelical one.

CHAPTER TWELVE

From Shoa to Shalom
The case for abolishing war in the twenty-first century

I. M. Gerald Goldberg

I: THE SETTING

In his recent exhibition (Galway, August 2003) Irish sculptor John Behan exhibited an elegant bronze piece of one of his favourite and most attractive subjects, birds, entitled *Doves on the Fence*. How far the irony is intentional only he could explain. For people increasingly opposed to war as a justified moral solution to a political problem, 'doves' as distinct from 'hawks', the fence-sitting itself, refusing to engage with the problems which provoke war and with the need to seek alternatives, is no longer morally justified. This essay by a Catholic theologian in a work honouring an Irish Jewish lawyer, Gerald Goldberg, is also written in painful consciousness of the fence-sitting (at best) of so many Europeans, Catholic and other Christians, during the 1930s and the 1940s when Gerald Goldberg's fellow Jews were facing extinction. In that spirit the title 'From Shoa to Shalom' is intended to explore how such catastrophes must not only be avoided *(nie wieder)* but replaced by a version of the great Hebrew vision and promise of Shalom, which might be best translated not simply as peace but as 'flourishing together in community', comprising eventually the whole human community.

A further word on the origins of the theme. After some years of gestation, the American theologian Stanley Hauerwas of Duke University, Durham, North Carolina, and this author composed an *Appeal to Theologians and Religious Leaders* to work for the abolition of war and the development of alternatives during the twenty-first century. The appeal was presented at conferences at the University of Notre Dame, Indiana in September 2002, and at Maynooth in November 2002 and has been published subsequently. This essay is to some extent an expansion of that appeal with much more attention to traditional arguments for a just war, to the difficulties which any alternative has to face and to the process and stages by which such an alternative might be introduced.

The controversy over the justification of the Iraq war, before and after its occurrence, has given a fresh edge to the debate and a new relevance to the project of abolishing war. Similar ideas and movements are beginning to develop around the world among ordinary people, politicians and even military personnel, as well as among the 'usual suspects' of pacifists, radical Christians, womens' groups and other political activists. The Irish Anti-War Movement, which was at the centre of organising the protest against the recent war in Iraq, and which published the interesting volume *Irish Writers against the War*, also states: 'We want to play our part in building the international movement to stop all wars.' This has been the long-standing ambition of Pax Christi Ireland together with its international associates.

On the basis of his criticism of the war in Iraq and his stringent efforts to prevent it, Pope John Paul II would seem to come very close to outlawing all war in the present world context. His phrase in the encyclical *Centesimus Annus* (1991), 'War never again', an exact echo of Pope Paul VI's remark at the United Nations in 1967, suggests that at that level of leadership the Catholic Church may be committing itself to the abolition of war as a moral instrument in extreme circumstances. For such a stance to be credible, church leaders in common with all other promoters of outlawing war will have to devote time and resources to the elaboration of alternatives and to the persuasion of its members who are also influential as citizens, politicians and military.

This, however, is not another appeal by a theologian to religious leaders or theologians, whatever their value in the overall project. One significant theologian in the debate, Professor Hans Küng of Tubingen, has argued that there can be no peace between the nations without peace between the religions. In many parts of the world, from Northern Ireland to the Middle East to South East Asia and beyond this argument seems to have much validity. It may be useful to return to this point later. The more central concern here is to examine the continuing usefulness and validity of just war theory and practice in today's globalising world and the feasibility of providing other solutions to the neuralgic problems of national security and sovereignty, of local conflict and global terrorism.

Writing in an Irish setting in honour of a distinguished Irish citizen, it is impossible to avoid the topic of Irish neutrality.

Without engaging with the tangled history of the underlying theory and actual practice of Irish neutrality, it may be that the implications of the abolition project may allow an Irish foreign policy which honours both its traditional stance of neutrality, still cherished it seems by very many Irish citizens, and its new commitments to European security and global peace. At least this is worth considering in face of the emotional and divisive controversy which some unimaginative proposals for dismantling neutrality and some rigid interpretations in retaining it may provoke.

II: THE ARGUMENTS

Just war and its limitations

The just war theory is not in its origins Christian. It existed at least in embryonic form and in varying versions among the Hebrew prophets as well as among the Greek and Stoic philosophers. It was known to Greek, Roman and other political and military leaders prior to its adoption by Christians in the fourth century of the Common Era (CE). There is a certain irony in its adoption and particularly in its widespread propagation by Christians, given that in their first three centuries they had rejected war and bearing arms as contrary to the teaching and example of their founder Jesus Christ.

Several summary conclusions may be drawn from the long and controversial development of just war theory and practice within the (Christian) West over 1500 years. The arguments about just war became increasingly complicated in face of the increasing complexity of military arms and their modes of delivery, from hatchets and spears to bows and arrows to guns and cannonry to bombs, conventional, atomic and nuclear, and from foot-soldiers to horses to battleships and motor vehicles to tanks, from jet-fighters and bombers to rocket launchers. Medieval debates about the moral legitimacy of bows and arrows were mirrored in similar debates about the use of gunpowder centuries later, down to the latter-day debates about cluster bombs and landmines to atomic, biological and chemical weapons. While the moral hesitations and debates about new weaponry may have had some restraining influence from time to time, as theologians and moralists attempted to refine the traditional *jus in bello* which presumed to impose moral limits on the actual conduct of war, morality and international law usually arrived too late, reflecting, like the infamous generals, the lessons of the last wars rather than examining in detail the new challenges of conduct in current or imminent wars.

Allowing for the later arrival of many moral and legal restrictions on the conduct of war, it remains sadly true that few if any historical wars have abided by the already established canons of morality or legality in the conduct of war. The best-case scenario of recent times, World War II as undertaken and conducted by the Allied Forces against the Nazi and Fascist regimes led, it is frequently asserted, through the carpet bombing of German cities and the atomic bombing of Japanese cities, to clear violation of the respect for non-combatants demanded by one traditional criterion for just conduct in war. It is at least debatable how far claims for precision bombing and the euphemistic invocation of unavoidable collateral damage in recent wars have given much real protection to non-combatants, especially when there have also been hospitals, communication centres, bridges and other civilian installations directly targeted and destroyed. One fairly safe generalisation from the history of wars might be that there never has been a war in which non-combatants have not been extensively killed and wounded. On that criterion alone wars have proved mainly unjust and perhaps unjustifiable. The qualifiers 'mainly' and 'perhaps' will be considered later in discussing some of the other criteria.

The counterweight to *jus in bello* was and is *jus ad bellum*. For many defenders of just war this is the primary, and for some the only significant criterion for a just war. In the fourth and fifth centuries CE, when the Christian theologian-bishops, Ambrose and Augustine, were pioneering the Christian theological justification of war and urging Christians to join the imperial armies, their argument was based on the need to defend the neighbours, Roman citizens, against the fearsome incursions of the barbarians who later managed to sack Rome itself. Defence against unjust and deadly aggression was their just cause and the first criterion advanced in moral argument. In his classic historical-theological analysis of just war theory over the centuries, Princeton theologian Paul Ramsey proposed, with considerable scholarly acuity, that the fourth-century change in Christian theory and practice and its subsequent development, arose out of the Hebrew and Christian command of love of neighbour with the consequent entailment to protect her/his life against unjust aggressors. Even in the tumultuous days of the Vietnam war and of the opposition to it, Ramsey stayed with his love of neighbour and her defence as justifying war. Today's Western rhetoric in support of particular wars is seldom far removed from that sentiment, even if the language is more of defence of freedom than of love of neighbour.

The justice of the cause has been the primary criterion in seeking to justify going to war but it has been gradually qualified by a number of related criteria. These involve what is nowadays called proportionality between the evil threatened and that which will inevitably ensue in war and by reasonable prediction of what may be expected to follow the war. Too often war has simply bred more war and that lesson seems very difficult for political and military leaders to absorb. How far did the Great War and its resolution at Versailles lead to the rise of Nazism and so to the catastrophes of World War II and of the Holocaust? The success of that war in ending the Nazi and Fascist tyrannies was clearly not of obvious benefit to the Poles, for example, whose invasion by Nazi Germany prompted the Allied declaration of war. It must also be remembered that protection of the Jews faced with genocide played little or no role in the declaration and conduct of the war despite growing awareness of the threat to the Jews through the nineteen thirties into the war years. All this emphasises the ambiguities of war in its initiation, continuance and conclusion.

Just cause as primary criterion is also restricted by the demand to engage in war only when all other means of averting the existing or threatened evil have been exhausted. This is obviously not an easy judgement to make as the heated and inconclusive debates about further inspections of Iraq's weapons of mass destruction, their threat to their neighbours or to the wider world and how best to deal with any such threat, made clear. In a more dynamic view of 'last-resort' commitment to extend alternative means to war now and into the future might at least give further pause to the trigger happy who are easily seduced by the prospect of 'shock-and-awe' solutions to long and near intractable problems. Again the aftermath of military victory in Iraq suggests alternatives might have been more earnestly and imaginatively sought and/or consequences and their tackling more fully thought through before the decision to go to war was finally made.

In this context the prospect and meaning of success in war enter into the equation. What should count as success in a particular war? Saving a small country like Poland from a tyrannical neighbour? Preserving the people of Vietnam from the horrors of communism? Discovering and destroying Saddam's weapons of mass destruction? Change of regime in Iraq? Liberating the Iraqi people? Promoting peace and democracy in the region? Further victory in the 'war against terrorism'? Securing Western interests, particularly in relation to oil? All of these questions about recent wars do not admit of ready, and certainly not agreed, answers even among allied states and statesmen. They do serve to underline again the ambiguities of war in its intentions and achievements and whisper at least, 'there must be a better way'.

Beneath and beyond the whispering there is a growing belief and increasing clamour that human beings must find alternatives to war in resolving political conflict and providing for human security. This widespread conviction is no longer satisfied with the niceties of just war theory and the awfulness of its practice. For many thoughtful people around the world, war is the last of the great social barbarisms and should follow slavery, torture and other historical barbarisms into moral and legal oblivion. Before that can happen a great deal of careful social and political analysis, as well as innovative and creative social and political change in mindset, structure and practice, will be demanded. No one essay, indeed no one theoretical dissertation, however lengthy, could hope to chart such analysis and changes. In these matters praxis frequently anticipates theory, experimentation settled programmes. All that will take time. The hope must be that the twenty-first century will witness the abolition of war as a moral and lawful instrument of politics as the nineteenth century witnessed the abolition of slavery as a moral and lawful instrument of economics. The continuing existence of slavery or enslavement in disguised or more limited forms does not give it any legal respectability or protection. One can no longer use as a legal or moral defence the concept of 'just slavery'. No doubt political recourse to arms in disguised or limited fashion will continue also but without the protection of international law or traditional morality.

III: ALTERNATIVES:
THEIR FOUNDATIONS, THEIR POSSIBILITIES AND THEIR DIFFICULTIES

In the appeal to theologians and others, the arguments for the abolition of war were primarily religious and the theologians involved mainly Christian. As indicated earlier this is a different kind of essay. However, any discussion on war and its alternatives has to take account of the formative religious traditions of Judaism and Christianity, particularly in the Western world, home and source of the most destructive weaponry and war the world has known. The God to whom Gideon in the Book of Judges dedicates an altar as to the Lord of Peace (Jdg 6:24) is hymned most beautifully in Psalm 84:

I will hear what the Lord God has to say,
a voice that speaks of peace,
peace for his people and his friends
and those who turn to him in their hearts.

Mercy and faithfulness have met;
justice and peace have embraced.
Faithfulness shall spring from the earth
and justice looks down from heaven.

The Lord will make us prosper
and our earth shall yield its fruit.
Justice shall march before him
and peace shall follow his steps.

The close connections revealed here between the ambitions of the Lord for his people and his creation and the corresponding divine and human attributes, peace *(shalom)*, justice *(sedeqah)*, mercy/loving kindness *(hesed)*, faithfulness *(emeth)* and prosperity and fruitfulness of the earth, summarise the characteristics of the Messianic age so often announced by the prophets. And the key feature of that age is shalom, the fullness of peace, best rendered in English perhaps as 'flourishing in community'. All of this in ambition and actuality is of course still embedded in a sinful and destructive world until the Messiah comes and the reign or kingdom of God is finally established.

For Christians the Messiah has already come in Jesus Christ. The reign of God is at hand. It has been established in principle for all people but must be accepted in love and pursued in prac-

tice by all justice-seekers and peace-makers who are addressed
as disciples by Jesus in his charter for the reign of God, the
Sermon on the Mount, and in other passages and parables. For
many Christians over the millennia Jesus' teaching and example
was enough to outlaw war, while they sought with more or less
energy and success to devise alternatives. In the present debate
such Christians need no other authority for their opposition to
war, while ironically many followers of the one God / Yahweh /
Allah, through adherence to Moses, Jesus and Mahomet in the
three Abrahamic faiths, may be the most resistant to the proposal
to abolish war.

In the course of the twentieth century three seriously religious people led the way in theory and practice in the search for
alternatives to violence and war in opposing the oppression of
their peoples and providing the freedom so rhetorically in
vogue in the West. Beginning with Gandhi in the 1890s in South
Africa and later India, emerging in mid-century in the USA with
Martin Luther King and reaching a climax in the Republic of
South Africa in the 1990s with Nelson Mandela, the philosophy
and political strategy of non-violent defence of neighbour, and
restraint of the armed aggressor and oppressor, opened up new
possibilities of achieving justice, freedom and security for all
kinds of people.

Gandhi, the most original thinker and actor among these
leaders, drew on his own Hindu tradition with its enormous respect for all living creatures, Jesus' Sermon on the Mount and its
teaching on love of enemies, and on the broader moral traditions
with their emphasis on truth, justice and freedom. His priority
on firmness in the truth (*satyagraha*) as the counter to armed
force or violence was put to the test many times by himself and
his *Satyagrahi*, those who stood firm in the truth and refused to
meet violence with violence. *Emeth*, the Hebrew word for truth
and faithfulness in truth, a particular characteristic of Yahweh
and his loyal people, has much in common with Gandhi's concept and practice. Neither has much in common with the propa-
ganda and spin of warring nations. The old adage retains its validity: the first casualty of war is truth. Gandhi's belief and his
partial achievement was that by continuing to expose the truth
of violence, oppression and injustice such as that experienced by
Indians and Africans at the hands of their white masters, and by
enduring the suffering which attempts to expose and uphold

that truth would inevitably bring, the masters would be eventually compelled by public disapproval, national and personal
shame, if not by conscience, to desist from their violence. In pursuit of his goals Gandhi realised that his *satyagrahi* needed careful preparation and training if they were to survive the rigours
of the campaign and resist the temptation to counter-violence.
Beyond that, he was as calculating a strategist in planning his
exposure campaigns, protest marches and fasting periods as any
top military general. The limited but undoubted success his
campaigns achieved in the liberation of India revealed the
strengths and weaknesses of such a programme in face of deep
ethnic and religious divisions and the usual practice of empire
to exploit such divisions to retain mastery. Gandhi's insight that
a successful programme such as his would lead to mutual emancipation for British master as well as Asian underling was too
much for most of his contemporaries, Indian perhaps as well as
British. And it exposes another harsh dimension of the war-
game, the dehumanising effect it has on the players, from generals in their combat centres to foot soldiers on the ground. The
false heroics of war were well known to Gandhi from the horrors of the Great War. His firmness in the truth would expose
the falsity of all such glorifying of war and liberate both sides
into possibilities of reciprocal justice and peace.

While Ghandhi's vision and practice inspired to good effect
such powerful disciples as Martin Luther King and Nelson
Mandela, and indeed John Hume and colleagues in Northern
Ireland, it has yet to capture much support in the West among
the political classes. Of course it would not on its own be adequate to the long, slow process of providing alternatives to war
around the globe. It could prompt the first essential step, the
change in mindset which is so badly needed among the warrior-
political classes which tend by inclination or indifference to
dominate discussion of issues such as freedom and security.
Interestingly, justice seldom figures in the vocabulary of these
people, still captive to the old Roman imperial tag: *si vis pacem,
para bellum*. If you desire peace, prepare for war. Talk of defend-
ing by war 'the free world' in such a deeply unjust world is as
misleading as it is futile. For the coming non-imperial times, one
hopes, the new tag might read: *si vis pacem, para justitiam*. If you
desire peace, prepare for justice. That is the change in mindset
that is immediately required. No peace without justice and finally
no justice without peace.

Changing mindsets at leadership and popular level will be slow and painful and always incomplete. It will help and be helped by short-term strategies in relieving glaring injustices, between developed western countries and the developing or impoverished countries of Africa, Asia and Latin America. That will involve changes in economic structures and practices which will demand serious commitment to fair trade in ways not yet shown by the economic powers, and the political will to impose such fairness if necessary. All the while international institutions will need to be strengthened in ways that ensure a growing body of just international law and effective means for its enforcement. These recommendations, which could and should be extended by the relevant experts, may appear at best obvious and banal, at worst naïve. What about national security? Humanitarian interventions? Disarmament and the elimination of the arms trade and industry? And so on. All these must be addressed and acted upon in ways that avoid, prevent or at least reduce in the short term the horror and inhumanity all war involves. Time and patience certainly, no easy and quick fix but commitment and urgency also for the sake of the next generation, and the next, and the next … who may die of war or injustice or both.

In seeking to move on from war and genocide to a just and peaceful human community, from Shoa to Shalom, mistakes will be made by so-called realists and idealists. It is difficult sometimes to tell the one from the other. Are the so-called hawks of world politics really realists? Do their understanding of the world and their prescription for its development and security offer any real hope of success? Are those just idealists who would, mind by mind, structure by structure, practice by practice, day by day, month by month, year by year and decade by decade seek the promotion of justice, the reduction and eventual elimination of political violence beyond the international police forces which will always be needed to protect the peace and security of an international and equal if still very different citizenry?

Naïve may be the easy accusation of the comfortable and powerful faced with such a disturbing project as the abolition of war. Yet there may be competing naïveties here. The naïvety of those who, in spite of continuing failure to establish justice and peace by war, still persist in the old prescriptions may be the more dangerous in the times ahead.

PART FOUR

In Art

CHAPTER THIRTEEN

Hopkins I: Vulnerable to the Holy

In the rich and complex context of this International School* and of the whole world of Hopkins scholarship, a few disclaimers are in order. This is clearly not the work of a literary critic or a historical study of the poet-Jesuit. And although my official competence is theology I would hesitate to call it a theological work. It is perhaps a meditative reflection on some poems of Hopkins, windhovering somewhere between aesthetic reaction and the preliminaries to prayer. Not a very precise category then.

Some general justification for this approach derives from a long-held conviction that one of the ways into prayer is through poetry and other artistic creations, and not necessarily what might be called religious poetry or art. In brief I suggest that the attention, concentration and eventually contemplation which a serious work of art elicits from the readers / viewers, draw them beyond themselves into an encounter which may open them up to a further, even transcendent presence. Despite the strictures of some post-modernist critics, contemporary intellectuals like George Steiner in his *Real Presences* and poet-critics like the recently deceased Elizabeth Jennings in *Every Changing Shape*, powerfully endorse a long tradition of connecting while distinguishing art and the transcendent, poetry and prayer.

Much of this has already no doubt been discussed at earlier sessions at this year's school which unfortunately I was unable to attend. Perhaps a more distinctive note may be struck by my alternative title and its implications. In preference to the title on the published programme, *Hopkins and Spirituality*, I have chosen, without I believe betraying the intent of the programme, to call my lecture, *Vulnerable to the Holy*, with the subtext of *Meditating on Poems of Gerard Manley Hopkins*.

Spirituality, in spite of or perhaps because of its widespread

* Lecture to the Hopkins International Summer School, Monasterevan, July 2003.

popularity, is not an easy term to manage nowadays. The indefinite range of meanings and applications which it enjoys can lead to a confusion or a vagueness which hinder real dialogue. Of course these difficulties may apply to many other words relevant to this discourse such as love, beauty, transcendence and even the holy. In fidelity to Hopkins one must try to use all words in as precise and clear a sense as possible without losing their contextual resonances. No mean ambition in the world of metaphor, analogy and perhaps mysticsm, the world of poetry, prayer and the holy.

Reader and poet: sharing a background?
In face of any poem or work of art, the backgrounds of poet and reader / viewer are influential, consciously or unconsciously, but never simply determining. (Please forgive the amateur's emphasis on what to the literary critic is so obvious.) In the present instance the Christian / Catholic background of the poet and of the reader / mediator at least overlap. One cannot say simply shared because Catholicism, the term Hopkins would prefer to use, is never simply monolithic over time or indeed over individuals at any one time. Hopkins himself is witness to this in his attachment to Duns Scotus in preference to Thomas Aquinas, the official theologian of the Jesuit order at that time. However, basic Christian beliefs in God as one and three, in creation and incarnation, in redemption and resurrection through Jesus Christ are shared by Catholics then as now, by this poet and this reader / meditator. Differences of perspective, insight and experience transfigured by the genius of the poet are to be taken for granted, yet the substance of Catholic belief provides the basis for further prayerful meditation for the least of Hopkins' Catholic readers. And not only for Catholic readers. As this school attests year by year, readers without Catholic faith or background can enjoy, appreciate and, I have no doubt, at times contemplate prayerfully the richness of Hopkins' poetry.

In his unusual essay on Hopkins' sanctity, poet Robert Lowell, while acknowledging the role in Catholic theology of sanctifying grace, goes on 'to emphasise ... that for Hopkins life was a continuous progress towards perfection. He believed this, he lived this, this is what he wrote.' And this is what in Lowell's opinion distinguished him from 'such great writers ... highly religious in their fashion' as 'Pope, Wordsworth, Coleridge,

Arnold or Browning'. Lowell's stress on perfection, on being 'in act' as characteristic of sanctity, at least of Hopkins' sanctity, reflects Catholic orthodoxy as far as it goes, but to leave aside further discussion of the role of grace as 'a digression' reinforces a rather lopsided view of holiness in that tradition. The primacy of grace, of the transforming presence and power of God, of the Transcendent, of the Holy provides the critical starting and finishing points for Hopkins as for the Catholic tradition in general. It provides the starting and finishing points for this Hopkins reader also.

More of the theological subtleties in the divine-human encounter will emerge in this meditation. The attracting, empowering and perfecting/transforming presence of God equivalent to the *gratia praeveniens, gratia concomitans* and *gratia perficiens* of Hopkins' theological education form the basis for the Ignatian concept of 'mutual election' between God and the individual so significant in Hopkins' Jesuit life. Against this background, emphasis on his personal striving for poetic, moral and religious perfection on the Lowell model may be more acceptable and for this reader make meditation more feasible.

'that being indoor each one dwells'
Duns Scotus' insight into the singularity of each individual famously changed Hopkins' vision of every person, object, landscape with its unique if transient self. This is brilliantly expressed in the first eight lines of this sonnet, a poem he expressed himself dissatisfied with. This may be because the concluding sestet is weaker poetically as the religious dimension emerges too quickly and too easily. For the meditating reader this may be a limitation also but he has still much to gain, much to be transformed by, as he surrenders to the exhilarating vision and music of the first four lines.

As kingfishers catch fire, dragonflies draw flame;
As tumbled over rim in roundy wells
Stones ring; like each tucked string tells, each hung bell's
Bow finds tongue to fling out broad its name.

The 'philosophical' comments in lines 5 and 6 articulate his Scotist position in language and rhythm very much his own.
Each mortal thing does one thing and the same:
Deals out that being indoors each one dwells;

Selves – goes itself; myself it speaks and spells,
Crying what I do is me; for that I came.

Scotus on the individual joins with scriptural words of Christ
to echo Lowell's description in the essay cited earlier of the
dramatic self-enactment by Hopkins of what he believed, lived
and wrote.

Of course Scotus' view on the relation between incarnation
and creation already hinted at emerges more clearly in the sestet
as the human being is not only God's creature but also Christ,
God's Son, who

plays in ten thousand places,
Lovely in limbs, and lovely in eyes not his
To the Father through the features of men's faces.

The self, the other and the holy

Whatever limitations Hopkins discerned in this poem, it offers a
summary of many of Hopkins' poetical and religious insights to
the meditative reader. For this reader it also offers an opportunity
to invoke some of the lessons he has learned as a theologian en-
countering and meditating on a poem or other art-work.

The distinctive reality of the poem must be faced in all its irreducibility and not taken over or manipulated by the reader for
some extraneous purpose of her own. This may be described as
a conversion by the reader to the poem in itself, or even as the
reader's surrender to it. In another image the reader may be said
to be inhabited by the poem. These images seek to convey the
primacy of the reader's receptivity in face of the given, but it is
by no means a passive receptivity but an active and creative one
involving the reader's active feeling, intellect and above all
imagination, as well as her sensitivity to language and sound.
The preparation for such an enriching encounter will include the
reader's previous attention to similar work, his literary education generally and his reflective life-experience. The whole person as lived to this point will encounter the poem and, if the encounter goes beyond the surface, the whole person will be
changed by it just as the poet in bringing his experience, skills
and inspiration has been changed by composing the poem.

That rather laboured account of reading a serious poem is intended to illuminate all human encounters with art-objects and
natural objects, human persons and even with God. In all such

encounters the distinctiveness and integrity of the encountered
calls for recognition and respect. Such recognition and respect
come at a price, as the language of surrender has already indicated. The reader, the observer, the encounterer must yield to and
accept the encountered as an irreducibly different self, which
   'Deals out that being indoors each one dwells;
   Selves…'
That is what may be called the vulnerability of each person to
the different as encountered in poem, nature, person or even an
event like a shipwreck. The patience hymned elsewhere by
Hopkins relates also to accepting the penetrating existence of
the different selves as present or absent, as windhover exultant
or Binsey poplars felled or as tall nun christening 'her wild-
worst Best'.

The different self of the encountered is explored by some
contemporary philosophers like Levinas as the other. Vulnerable
to the other might well describe some of his ethical analysis. The
term and reality of the other has a long and distinguished lin-
eage within the Jewish and Christian traditions. In Hebrew
qadosh, the word for other, applied primarily to the utterly different, the absolutely other than creatures, the Creator, Yahweh,
God. And so qadosh was translated as holy, the absolutely other,
the Transcendent was the Holy One of Israel. In respect for his
presence in the burning bush on Mount Horeb, Moses must remove his shoes. The history of Israel becomes the history of the
Holy One as Lord of Creation and of his people Israel who are to
be a holy people set apart, living by a code of holiness with holy
places to be venerated and holy times and practices to be observed. And primary to that life must be regard and love for the
neighbour, the supreme image of the divine other. Without love
of neighbour, particularly of the poor and the marginalised, sac-
rifices to the Ultimate Other were a fraud to be rejected, as Amos
and his fellow-prophets insisted.

The otherness or holiness of God was manifest in all creation
but climactically in human beings. Beyond that in the Scotus-
Hopkins world, the incarnation took priority over creation and
Christ as the Word of God made flesh was at the heart of all
divine self-communication, the presence of the holy through
natural and human entities and events. Encounter with these entities and events enabled Hopkins to perceive their inscape and
instress in Christ, to appropriate that in his own personal and

poetic vision and to give it fresh instress and inscape in his poetry. So the attentive reader could replicate in her fashion the instress and inscape of the poem as a language entity and have mediated by meditation the poet's experience of human, natural reality and its Christ dimension, the Holy in its awesome, consoling and transforming power.

The beauty, the terror and the redeeming power

In his poetic responses to his Christ-filled world, Hopkins retained his sense of the uniqueness of each natural and human reality. The deeper Christ inscape of creation implied no hidden pantheism. The triune God of orthodox Christianity remained the ultimate other, the Holy One, while each creature retained that self/created other 'indoors each one dwells'. The tension generated by this vision of the world and its God provides much of the energy, beauty and mystery realised in the poems. It hints also at the pain of their creation as if Hopkins like Yeats, in Auden's phrase, had been hurt into poetry but not for the same reason of course; not by 'mad Ireland' but by the beauty and the terror which he experienced in his attempt to capture in words the pied beauty fathered forth by him 'whose beauty is past change' or 'that year/Of now done darkness I wretch lay wrestling with (my God!) my God'. Even in these dark sonnets he remains conscious of the finally redeeming power of God and advises his jaded soul to 'let joy size/At God knows when to God knows what ...'

Vulnerable to the holy in nature

Hopkins is rightly regarded as one of the great nature poets in the English language. In this context his eye focuses the Springscape: 'When weeds in wheels, shoot long and lovely and lush'; or one ear attends to 'the tide that ramps against the shore'; while the other 'hear the lark ascend, ... and pour/And pelt music, till none's to spend'. In the rich range of his nature poetry the vision crowds his eye while the music throngs his ear. In these experiences he becomes vulnerable and does poetic justice not only to the inscape and instress of this worldly world but 'to the dearest freshness deep down things; ... Because the Holy Ghost over the bent/World broods with warm breast and ah! bright wings'.

For Hopkins the Catholic, the beauty of creation reflects and

mediates the presence of the Creator God, the Holy One of Israel
and of Jesus Christ. In his poetry he never forgets that this creation 'is charged with the grandeur of God'. He emphasises that
in his grand appeal to 'Give beauty back to God, beauty, beauty,
beauty, back to God, beauty's self and beauty's giver'. For
Hopkins the disciple of Scotus, incarnation and creation were so
closely intertwined that the 'dapple-dawn-drawn falcon … in
his ecstasy' embodies Hopkins' 'hero' and 'chevalier', 'Christ
our Lord'. Open to nature in all its God-given beauty is to be
penetrated by or vulnerable to the Holy and 'God's better beauty
grace'.

A reminder of course that for all his appreciation of the beauty
of creation he was also aware of its distractions and dangers as
that last poem quoted indicated in title and content: 'To What
Serves Mortal Beauty?' The joy and pain of the holy were always
reaching through in even his most lyrical hymns to nature. 'The
world [that] is charged with the grandeur of God … is seared
with trade; bleared, smeared with toil;/And wears man's
smudge and shares man's smell …'

The felling of the Binsey Poplars continues the theme of
man's inhumanity to nature, of his unholy destruction of natural
beauty and its inscape of the holy: 'even where we mean/To
mend her we end her,/When we hew or delve:/Aftercomers
cannot guess the beauty been'. Human destructiveness is never
Hopkins' last word. While the inmate does not correspond to
'the woods, waters, meadows, combes, vales/All the air things
wear that build this world of Wales,' Hopkins prays, 'God, lover
of souls, swaying considerate scales,/Complete thy creature
dear O where it fails,/Being mighty a master, being a father and
fond'. As father and fond, God is vulnerable to the call to restore
the beauty neglected or distorted and to forgive the people ne-
glecting or distorting.

Brothers in beauty

In so many of his poems Hopkins shows himself vulnerable to
human beauty. Not unaware of its dangers ('To What Serves
Mortal Beauty') or its fragility ('Margaret, are you grieving'), he
cherished the beauty of the newly-wed in 'At the Wedding
March' and even more the beautiful, tender loving of the (blood)
'Brothers' on the night of the school play. In poems concerning
particular people, 'brothers [and sisters] in Christ', from Duns

Scotus to Henry Purcell to Felix Randal to Saint Alphonsus
Rodriguez to the Bugler Boy, Hopkins responded to their particular instress and inscape in a beautifully modulated way. For
Scotus and Purcell the intellectual intensity combined with complex word music to enable the reader to receive 'at a third remove' a sense of their gifts and of their influence on the poet. As
the poet is changed in the writing so is the reader in the reading
by conversion to the beauty and the holy which they embodied.
A simpler but still beautiful and, as this essay argues, holy
experience confronts the reader of the other personal poems
with their more overt religious connections. Again both poet
and reader are taken beyond themselves as in the first tercet of
'Felix Randal':

> This seeing the sick endears them to us, us too it endears.
> My tongue had taught thee comfort, touch had quenched thy
>   tears,
> Thy tears that touched my heart, child, Felix, poor Felix
>   Randal.

Thou mastering me/God

In any meditation on the poems of Hopkins and particularly in
one entitled Vulnerable to the Holy, 'The Wreck of the Deutschland' and the late dark, near despairing sonnets would seem to
constitute primary material. Where else is the vulnerability of
poetic matter and of poet so evident? One reason for hesitation
might be the danger of the reader being overwhelmed by the
volume and depth of the material. Another would be the
amount of scholarly, literary and even theological attention already devoted to these poems. They are after all in many people's opinion his supreme achievement. Reading and re-reading
them one is rendered at first speechless by 'the achieve of, the
mastery of the thing'. And these poems deserve much longer
and more insightful meditation than this occasion allows or this
amateur could attempt. Yet they cannot be ignored whatever the
limitation of reader and of occasion.

Most scholars agree that the first eleven stanzas of 'The
Deutschland' deal directly with Hopkins' personal life. (Indeed
one twentieth-century Dutch confrère of his believes it was composed after the narrative half dealing with shipwreck itself,
when Hopkins had as it were been penetrated by the inscape of
the story and could apply it to his own internal life.) At any rate

almost any stanza of these first eleven provides ample source for meditation on human vulnerability to the Holy in its awesome, creative and unmaking power. Perhaps we should listen again to the first four stanzas to appreciate something of the poet's terror of and ultimate consolation in the Holy, 'Christ's gift'.

The rest of the poem is a mine for such meditation and the originating theme and its powerful narration in part two permit endless variations on openness to the human as well as the ultimate other in all their terrifying and exultant strangeness and holiness.

Choosing a single sonnet from Hopkins' final despairing fling to match the theme of his being hurt into poetry by the Holy as threat or gift, in its absence or presence, is simply impossible. All these poems witness to the human suffering and its poetic transfiguration, if not all get as far as the hope and consolation of resurrection.

'No worst there is none' where 'the mind ... has mountains; cliffs of fall/Frightful, sheer, no-man-fathomed. Hold them cheap/May who ne'er hung there.' And 'Here! creep/Wretch, under a comfort serves in whirlwind'.

'Carrion Comfort' for all its foreboding title resists in obvious pain the temptation of Despair. Yet hurt at the hands of God, 'thou terrible', ... 'the hero whose heaven-handling flung me, foot trod/Me? Or me that fought him? O which one? is it each one? That night, that year/Of now done darkness I wretch lay wrestling with (my God!) my God.'

In the midst of such painful poetry and meditation the exhilarating music and final vision of that wonderful late poem 'That Nature Is A Heraclitean Fire and of the Comfort of the Resurrection' enables a triumph beyond all dark, drowning and destruction by fire.

In a flash, at a trumpet crash,
I am all at once what Christ is, since he was what I am, and
This Jack, joke, poor potsherd, patch, matchwood, immortal
    diamond,
Is immortal diamond.

What Christ is, the Christ now of resurrection as well as crucifixion, the Christ who experienced abandonment on the cross but whose vulnerability to the Holy, to the Father, liberated us all from the darkness, the darkness that came over the earth from the sixth to the ninth hours in Mark's words, liberated us into the brilliant and everlasting light of immortal diamond.

Wrestling with Hopkins' poems in meditation is one way of renewing and deepening our vulnerability to the holy in nature, humanity and God.

CHAPTER FOURTEEN

Hopkins II:
Reconciliation and Beauty*

In the course of a personal and professional life devoted to exploring and communicating the meaning of the moral life from a Christian perspective, I have sometimes been compelled to change course, in the broader sense of intellectual development as well as in the more technical sense of providing courses of study for students of Christian morality. I hope this has not involved too many inconsistencies or u-turns. I would naturally prefer to see the changes as extension and deepening in my understanding of the Christian and indeed human way of life. On this occasion I wish to concentrate on two prompters of that development, namely poetry (and the arts generally) and politics. In pursuit of this task I will focus on a particular exemplar of a poet and poetry who continues to nourish these developments, Gerard Manley Hopkins, and on political engagement, particularly reconciliation, and on how they might interact in enriching, even in transforming the moral imagination of this time.

A few preliminary clarifications may be helpful before undertaking the central tasks. Much moral analysis, religious and secular, past and present, concentrates on too narrow a grasp of the reality to be analysed and with too restricted a concept of the analysing mind or person. Human relations with one another or with the planet earth are frequently the subject of a rational calculus of consequences in terms of material benefits, while ignoring the incalculable dimensions of all human and earthly realities accessible to the imagination, celebrated by artists and at the limit to be accepted as mystery. Even the essential and liberating moral language of human rights, which must be ultimately founded in the irreducible, mysterious character of each human being, is not adequate to the subtleties of human relations in such basics as trust, friendship and political reconciliation. Religious discourse on morality is no less open to the temptation of reducing morality by a fundamentalist concentration on di-

148

*Lecture at University of Melbourne, October 2003.

vine imperatives as mediated literally and uncritically by biblical text or church authority. These limitations in secular and religious moral discourse, with their destructive implications in
practice, are due to the failures of the human imagination to
comprehend the richness, diversity and mystery of the human
and earthly condition. Meditating on some of the poetry of
Gerard Manley Hopkins, as on other significant poetry, can
nourish and expand that imagination in ways unimaginable to
too many moralists.

Meditating is the key. Unable to assume the role of literary
critic and unwilling to reduce the poetry to moral lessons, one
must listen and grow by letting the poems take over, by surrendering to them, by letting them inhabit one. How far in this instance the practice is successful for the meditator or his audience
cannot be predicted beforehand. At the risk of letting the preliminaries dominate the main act, it might be useful to invoke the
recent renewal of an ancient church practice, that of *lectio divina*
or divine reading. In its contemporary and more sophisticated
form, the *lectio divina* offers a prayerful context for communal
reading, listening to and meditating on the divine scriptures of
the Jewish and Christian traditions. Cardinal Martini, himself a
notable scripture scholar, promoted this practice very effectively
particularly with young people in the 1980s and 1990s when
Archbishop of Milan. What is proposed here is rather a *lectio
humana*, a reading of human scriptures which, as listened to in
meditative fashion, expand the listener beyond any immediate
and prosaic world into that encountered and expressed by the
artist. Where this expansion ceases depends on poet/poem and
reader/listener.

A poet of such intense religious sensibility as Hopkins is in
danger of being misread and misrepresented by people of strong
religious convictions but of little poetic sensibility or education.
For them Hopkins would be at best a symbol of Catholic success
in a hostile, secular context as Marshall MacLuhan hinted all
those years ago. At worst his work could be manipulated in
some propagandist cause. The non-religious, quick to pro-
nounce himself baffled by the overt religious references, may be
tempted to dismiss the poetry as no more than religious verse
with a propagandist intent. It is not easy being a religious artist
in a dominantly secular world, an artist who would have his art
taken seriously as art. For that and other reasons many contem-

porary artists with a strong spiritual sense of humanity and the world elect to proceed indirectly and implicitly in so far as religious tradition and doctrine is concerned. This poetic strategy may be no less authentic than the more explicit work of somebody like Hopkins and no less transforming in the *lectio humana* practice described earlier.

In reading and listening to Hopkins' poems, and he would have them read aloud and listened to in the conventional sense as he insisted in his letters to Robert Bridges and other friends, in reading and listening to these poems then their very strangeness in sound and style, in syntax and rhythm, even in language is demanding. A Hopkins poem will often take many readings and listenings, parallel no doubt to the much labouring, in Yeats' phrase, which the writing of a good poem involves. For ever since Adam's fall, in the Yeats version, 'we must labour to be beautiful' and, one might add, oft times to appreciate the beautiful. In this context the poem itself, in its strangeness and uniqueness, presents a challenge to which the reader should surrender rather than seek to master.

A number of images and analogies relevant to the role of reader and of poet could be illuminating here. As the reader surrenders to the poem, s/he may come to be inhabited and so transformed by it as indicated earlier. This might also be described in terms of conversion, the conversion of the reader to the world of the poem. This of course operates at the imaginative and aesthetic levels and not primarily at the moral and religious levels, although such conversions may follow later. At least the reader will be opened to the different world of the poem, to its distinctive otherness and so extended and changed in ways analogous to how the poet was extended and changed in composing the poem. It is in this imaginative openness to the other and its beauty that the moral capacity is enriched, perhaps originates. One of the great moral philosophers of the twentieth century, Emmanuel Levinas, regarded the challenge of the other, indeed the face of the human other, as the source of all moral demand/responsibility. By extending this regard for the other to the poem as well as the person, to the particular event as well as natural world in all its rich diversity, one may see how the moral imagination is significantly enlarged and strengthened. In the poems of Hopkins all these realities, poem and person, historical event and natural phenomenon have the capacity to challenge and transform the reader.

Nature revealed

Hopkins is rightly regarded as one of the great nature poets in the English language. The poem 'Pied Beauty' is one of his best known and most popular nature poems. It emphasises, as most of his nature poems do, that the beauties of nature derive from the Creator-God and that God's beauty. Yet the distinctive beauty of the poem and the multiple beauties of nature with their own distinctive patterns, or inscapes as Hopkins would call them, are respected and cherished for what they are in themselves.

Pied Beauty

Glory be to God for dappled things –
For skies of couple-colour as a brinded cow –
For rose-moles all in stipple upon trout that swim;
Fresh-firecoal chestnut-falls; finches' wings;
Landscape plotted and pieced – fold, fallow and plough;
And all trades, their gear and tackle and trim.

All things counter, original, spare, strange;
Whatever is fickle, freckled (who knows how?)
With swift, slow; sweet, sour; adazzle, dim;
He fathers-forth whose beauty is past change;
    Praise him.

The painterly and musical qualities of this poem, with its exacting visual observation and its musical verbal expression, are characteristic of all Hopkins' nature poetry and reflects his incipient talents and ambitions as would-be painter and musical composer. The *lectio humana* mentioned earlier as called for by serious literary work is linked in reading Hopkins to a *visio* and *musica humana*, a human vision and music which enable the reader to surrender to the complex and beautiful pattern of the poem, its inscape. As the poet has surrendered to these beauty-patterns of nature, their inscape as 'dappled' in 'skies of couple-colour', 'Fresh-firecoal chestnut-falls', 'All things counter, original, spare strange', he draws the reader into the sense of the extraordinary diversity of nature, and despite that diversity and the contrasts, even conflicts involved, 'swift, slow; sweet, sour; adazzle, dim', they are reconciled in the poem by the creator-poet as in the world by the Creator-God.

Few poets attempt such dazzling and innovative/creative contrasts of language as Hopkins. In this he was consciously re-

newing the language while at the same time healing it of its
wearisome tawdriness. In another image, he could be said to
play a reconciling role in his choice of words and of the realities
they sought to present to the reader. With his technical and artistic genius he was letting words play off one another rather than
against one another, in a mode of reconciliation all the more significant because of his intense sense of the difference and
uniqueness of 'All things counter, original, spare, strange'.

Laboured reflections on the poems of Hopkins must continually return to reading and listening to the poems themselves.
This next poem belongs to his nature poetry with some interesting differences. It is a sonnet. Unlike 'Pied Beauty', Hopkins did
not give it a title. Robert Bridges, to whom we owe the first publication of Hopkins' poetry, used the first phrase as its title. Here
is the octet as it is called, the first eight lines of the sonnet:

> As kingfishers catch fire, dragonflies draw flame;
> As tumbled over rim in roundy wells
> Stones ring; like each tucked string tells, each hung bell's
> Bow swung finds tongue to fling out broad its name;
> Each mortal thing does one thing and the same:
> Deals out that being indoors each one dwells;
> Selves – goes itsself; *myself* it speaks and spells,
> Crying *What I do is me; for that I came.*

The vision and the music are as powerful as ever but the
philosophical reflection, if not too abstract a phrase, emerges
more clearly. 'Each mortal thing does one thing and the same.'
We must return to 'mortal' but the same: 'Deals out that being
indoors each one dwells'. The essence of a thing, natural and
human as here, historical and verbal elsewhere, its inscape is
dealt out as it 'Selves – goes itself'. This description of the partic-
ularity of each reality reveals something of Hopkins' discovery
of the philosophy of medieval scholar Duns Scotus with his notion of the 'thisness' (*haecceitas*) which as he (Hopkins) said
changed his vision of everything in the world. Such profound
differentiation, such otherness to use a contemporary term,
drew Hopkins into some of his most daring poetry and in other
moods left him with a sense of isolation bordering on desolation. In another untitled sonnet written in Ireland towards the
end of his life, he begins: 'To seem the stranger lies my lot'. But
those desperate poems must wait a while.

'Each mortal thing', the created world has as its climax the human being, also part of Hopkins' natural world. Dealing out that being indoors dwells 'the just man justices ... Acts in God's eyes what in God's eyes he is – Christ'. The primacy and centrality of incarnation, so essential to Scotus and to Hopkins, breaks through here as in so many of his great nature poems. It attains perhaps its supreme expression for Hopkins in his marvellously difficult poem, 'The Windhover', which he dedicates 'To Christ our Lord'.

Some images and phrases in that poem remind the reader of the sweeping beauty of Hopkins' own celebratory poetry; 'striding/High there, how he rung upon the rein of a wimpling wing/In his ecstasy'. Any reader's 'heart in hiding' would stir for 'the achieve of, the mastery of the thing', the poem. But the ecstasy and the achieve of bird or poet were not without their shadow side. Hopkins' sense of the limitations of natural and mortal beauty and of the damage inflicted on nature by humanity itself figured in many of his best poems. 'Binsey Poplars' might provide nourishment for the moral imagination of the Greens of today, as they seek to awaken global consciousness to human destruction of the environment, not on some utilitarian basis but as respect for nature in itself, in its instress and beauty.

Binsey Poplars

My aspens dear, whose airy cages quelled,
Quelled or quenched in leaves the leaping sun,
All felled, felled, are all felled;
Of a fresh and following folded rank
Not spared, not one
That dandled a sandalled
Shadow that swam or sank
On meadow and river and wind-wandering weed-winding
    Bank

O if we but knew what we do
When we delve or hew –
Hack and rack the growing green!
Since country is so tender
To touch, her being so slender,
That, like this sleek and seeing ball
But a prick will make no eye at all,
Where we, even where we mean
To mend her we end her,

When we hew or delve:
After-comers cannot guess the beauty been.
Ten or twelve, only ten or twelve
Strokes of havoc unselve
The sweet especial scene,
    Rural scene, a rural scene,
    Sweet, especial rural scene.

The theme of human indifference and injury to the beauty about it is a frequent theme of Hopkins. He sings of the natural beauty 'In the Valley of the Elwy'; 'Lovely the woods, waters, meadows, combes, vales,/All the air things wear that build this world of Wales./Only the inmate does not correspond.' 'All this juice and all this joy' in the poem 'Spring' is 'A strain of the earth's sweet being in the beginning/In Eden garden' 'Before it cloud ... and sour with sinning'. Human sin not only spoils the beauty of creation as charged with the grandeur of God, it renders that very beauty itself dangerous as he announces in a short poem, 'To what serves Mortal Beauty?' And that mortality itself sets young Margaret grieving 'Over Goldengrove unleaving' when it's really over 'the blight man was born for/It is Margaret you mourn for'.

These and other laments for the transience and mortality of natural and human beauty are not simple qualifications of his earlier enthusiasms but part of a persistent dialectic between the intensity of his vision of that beauty and that of his vision of its tragic fragility. Out of such dialectic are authentic art and ethics frequently born. That dialectic sways this way and that throughout Hopkins' work. Indeed in his very first work to be written as a Jesuit, and which established him to himself as the major poet he became, 'The Wreck of the Deutschland', the tragic seemed to dominate, as it did in his last great sonnets of desolation if not desperation.

In 'The Deutschland' Hopkins, for our purposes, takes on two major tasks of aesthetics, ethics and religion; how to deal with tragedy in a way that is both honest to the horrors and transformingly if painfully beautiful for the reader; and how to cope with the problem of such disaster afflicting good and innocent people while believing in a loving providence. In the presence of catastrophe the imagination itself may quail. Who could write poetry, or do theology for that matter, in the aftermath of the Holocaust? was a question frequently posed in the 1950s and 60s. The more limited disasters of 9/11 in New York or of last year in Bali could raise similar difficulties. And in my own more direct experience, the ravages of the pandemic HIV/AIDS in sub-Saharan Africa leave one frequently and properly speechless. The wreck of the ship carrying passengers, including five Franciscan nuns expelled from Germany under the Falck laws from Bremen to the new world was not on such an epic scale. For Hopkins it was a profound tragedy which hurt him into his first poetry since joining the Jesuits. The scale was sufficient to draw him into an intense imaginative reconstruction of the ship's fate and at the same time an exploration of his own spiritual condition as he also explained to Bridges in a letter.

The opaqueness of the poem, which probably led his Jesuit confrère, editor of the journal *The Month*, to refuse it publication, and its length make it a more appropriate subject for a series of lectures and seminars than for the brief reference possible here. Yet some illustration of the imaginative daring of its descriptions and their transforming quality may help to see how beauty reaches beyond horror and how providence in Hopkins' vision is still at work.

Stanza XVI reads:
One stirred from the rigging to save
The wild woman-kind below,
With a rope's end round the man, handy and brave –
He was pitched to his death at a blow,
For all his dreadnought breast and braids of thew:
They could tell him for hours, dandled the to and fro
Through the cobbled foam-fleece. What could he do
With the burl of the fountains of air, buck and the flood of the
   wave?

XVII
They fought with God's cold –
And they could not and fell to the deck
(Crushed them) or water (and drowned them) or rolled
With the sea-romp over the wreck.
Night roared, with the heart-break hearing a heart-broke
   rabble,
The woman's wailing, the crying of a child without check –
Till a lioness rose breasting the babble,
A prophetess towered in the tumult, a virginal tongue told.

XIX
Sister, a sister calling
A master, her master and mine! –
And the inboard seas run swirling and hauling,
The rash smart sloggering brine
Blinds her; but she that weather sees one thing, one;
Has one fetch in her; she rears herself to divine
Ears, and the call of the tall nun
To the men in the tops and tackle rode over the storm's
    brawling.

XX
She was first of a five and came
Of a coif-ed sisterhood

XXIV
She to the black-about air, to the breaker, the thickly
Falling flakes, to the throng that catches and quails
Was calling 'O Christ, Christ, come quickly';
The cross to her she calls Christ to her, christens her wild-
    worst Best.

And for those without this courageous nun's faith and trust in
Christ they are:

No not uncomforted: lovely-felicitous Providence
Finger of a tender of, O of a feathery delicacy, the breast of the
Maiden could obey so, be a bell to ring of it, and
Startle the poor sheep back! is shipwrack then a harvest,
    does tempest carry the grain for thee?

The first section of the poem, stanzas I-XI was written, some
commentators think, after the second narrative part from which
we have been reading. It reflects very directly Hopkins' spiritual
condition. It also illustrated the deep internal connection between what we might call Hopkins the Mystic and Hopkins the
Poet, something at least implicit in his later nature and other
poetry. However, it may be more helpful at this stage to attend
to those other great poems of Hopkins, written in his last years
and sometimes described as his poems of desolation or even
desperation.

One of these poems quoted earlier, 'To seem the stranger', reflects his separation from England, family and friends but goes much deeper into his poetic desert.

> Only what word
> Wisest my heart breeds dark heaven's baffling ban
> Bars or hell's spell thwarts. This to hoard unheard,
> Heard unheeded, leaves me a lonely began.

The poetic desert is also a spiritual desert. Abandonment by God becomes the more piercing cry. Only somebody with Hopkins' intense experience of God as recorded earlier could now experience so intensely the pain of God's absence. The slow discovery of God in the 'Deutschland' poem, as Hopkins and the tall nun christen their wild worst best, escapes the Hopkins who cries in another of these sonnets:

> No worst, there is none. Pitched past pitch of grief,
> More pangs will, schooled at forepangs, wilder wring.
> Comforter, where, where is your comforting?
> Mary, Mother of us, where is your relief?
> My cries heave, herds-long; huddle in a main, a chief
> Woe, world-sorrow; on an age-old anvil wince and sing –
> Then lull, then leave off. Fury had shrieked 'No Lingering! Let me be fell; force I must be brief'.
>
> O the mind, mind has mountains; cliffs of fall
> Frightful, sheer, no-man fathomed. Hold them cheap
> May who ne' er hung there. Nor does long our small
> Durance deal with that steep or deep. Here! creep
> Wretch, under a comfort serves in a whirlwind: all
> Life death does end and each day dies with sleep.

The dark nights and days which Hopkins chronicles do not yield finally to despair:

> Not, I'll not, carrion comfort, Despair, feast on thee;

although he concludes the poem by recalling:

> That night, that year / Of now done darkness I wretch lay wrestling with (my God!) my God.

In the overpowering poem 'That Nature is a Heraclitean Fire and of the Comfort of the Resurrection' he expresses most ex-

plicitly from within the pain and the darkness, in the midst of
the world-sorrow, his Christian hope:

> Across my foundering deck [Deutschland again ?] shone
> A beacon, an eternal beam. Flesh fade, and mortal trash
> Fall to the residuary worm; world's wildfire, leave but ash;
> In a flash, at a trumpet crash,
> I am all at once what Christ is, since he was what I am, and
> This Jack, joke, poor potsherd, patch, matchwood, immortal
>   diamond,
> Is immortal diamond.

For critics, non-religious and religious, as I suggested earlier,
this ending may prove too strong for the poem and for all the
poems of desolation. The religious may just want to escape the
desolation and the poem into too easy acceptance of resurrection. The non-religious may dismiss the poem as mere *apologia*
for a conclusion already reached. That is why it is so important
to stay close to the poems and see how they explore authentically
the sorrows of the world and agony of the individual believer
whose God has abandoned him. Jesus' cry of abandonment on
the cross may have been Hopkins' final inspiration but the shaping of the poems, their agonised formation from the chaos of his
suffering to the cosmos of the finished poems are themselves
harbingers of hope. In a discussion of Philip Larkin's 'Aubade',
which he calls the first post-Christian poem in English, Seamus
Heaney finds Larkin not entirely despairing and rejecting of life
as the content of the poem might suggest. In Heaney' s view, if I
remember it correctly, the rhythm and music of the poem beat
out a counter-message affirming life. This would be my reading
of Hopkins' poems of desolation also although it was perhaps
inevitable that his poetry would finally uncover the Christian
sense of that hope in the immortal diamond of Christ.

From Chaos to Cosmos, to the beautiful God-guided order of
creation and resurrection in 'The Deutschland' and in the desperate sonnets, offers one perspective on Hopkins and one
model for the human creators of the beautiful and the good. The
beautiful and the good were celebrated in the rich diversity of
the nature poems and in the personal poems about the Bugler
Boy, Henry Purcell and others which we did not have time to consider. Yet in all these the very inscape of created realities, their
profound distinctiveness were drawn together in powerfully di-

verse words and phrases, rhymes and rhythms, another form not only of creation but of reconciliation in its original sense of bringing the truly different realities or others into living harmony. Such creation can provide ethical and political indicators of which I spoke earlier. In the Hopkins world his acute sense of the distinctive pattern of each thing, its inscape, relates to the otherness which forms the heart of the moral relationship. No morality without difference or otherness. Yet it is this very otherness or strangeness which renders morality risky, as the other may be interpreted as potentially enriching or potentially threatening, as gift or threat. In the reconciling activity the gift triumphs over the threat but never completely or permanently. So the work of reconciliation is a never-ending call in politics as well as in personal morality. In enabling the reader/meditator to understand the depths of difference, its potential threat and its potential goodness and beauty in reconciliation, Hopkins in his poetry has much to offer.

In conclusion, I wish to look briefly at two poems, extracts from Hopkins' unfinished play based on the legend of St Winifred which he came across while studying at St Beuno's, the Jesuit College in Wales. Winifred dedicates her life to God in prayer and chastity but is beheaded by Prince Caradoc who is obsessed with her beauty, when she rejects him. Where her head falls a holy well occurs which Hopkins visited. Perhaps intended for a musical setting with antiphonal chorus, 'The Leaden Echo' and 'The Golden Echo' as they are called, recall the reader/listener to Hopkins' awareness of the cosmos which may become chaos which may then become cosmos. The final call to humanity is to give beauty back to God.

In 'The Leaden Echo' there is nothing it seems to halt decay and the slide into despair:

O there's none; no no no there's none:
Be beginning to despair, to despair,
Despair, despair, despair, despair.

The Golden Echo follows

Spare!
There is one, yes I have one (Hush there!) ...
O why are we so haggard at the heart ...
When the thing we freely forfeit is kept with fonder a care ...

So the centre of our human and Christian vocation, in person, poetry and politics is to:

Give beauty back, beauty, beauty, beauty, back to God beauty's self and beauty's giver.

CHAPTER FIFTEEN

An Office of Readings

According to the blurb on the back cover, 'John F. Deane shapes his new collection, *Manhandling the Deity*, in a framework that calls to mind the Roman Catholic Mass, celebrated for the living and the dead.' Despite the deeply religious nature of its celebration of the living and the dead I am not sure that the overall framework of the collection is easily related to the shape of the Catholic Mass; certainly not in the way a Mozart Mass is or, a more relevant example, *Mass for Hard Times* by fellow-poet, R. S. Thomas. However, Deane's volume has a discernible liturgical feel and structure to it, most obviously in the *Officium* poems introducing each main section and in the closing poems, *Recessional* and *Canticle*. For this reader and perhaps others the variety of poetry, nature, love and explicitly religious poetry, may be enjoyed with another related interpretative key.

A liturgy of reading

In the recent rush to spirituality in a rather shallow secularist world, one of the better responses of Christians has been that known as the *lectio divina*. A form of meditation based on reading or better listening to the Hebrew and Christian scriptures, ancient in origin, *lectio divina* has developed new techniques of engagement which many people find increasingly attractive. For too many these scriptures are still a closed book and alternatives, serious and shoddy, from high art to new-age frivolity are readily available and eagerly availed of. A rather solemn introduction to a delightful and truly poetic work, John F. Deane's *Manhandling the Deity*. Yet even the book's title, formidable as it is, at once reveals and obscures my point. For many committed and searching Christians for whom the scriptural *lectio divina* is not immediately or permanently fulfilling, poetry among the arts can offer a significant spiritual alternative whether or not it leads to reading the scriptures or to any explicit Christian commitment. In this work, as in so many others, John Deane has multiple explicit and implicit Christian references manifesting a deep religious sensibility. His Manhandling of the Deity is in the tradition of stable birth and criminal execution. The beauty and music of language and image already herald the resurrection appropriate to his and indeed God's need to promote justice for our manhandling of the God and our mishandling of God's human family and world. Reading these poems aloud, as I prefer, or in silence, one is moved reflectively from the world of the *lectio naturalis et humana* of a true poet to at least the possibility of the *lectio divina* of the true God

All of this needs much further exploring. Here a three-fold division will also be followed but a rather different one from that of Deane in the collection itself. The first stage of the exploration and reading will concentrate on some of the nature poems and on what may be called a *lectio naturalis*. In the second stage the focus will be on poems dealing with specific human beings. This may be described as a *lectio humana*. In the final section the more explicitly religious poems will be considered. Of course none of these are what you might call pure forms. Nature, human beings and the deity intermingle in most of his work. However, it is helpful to look at poems where one or other of these themes predominates. And these distinctions are particularly important in a poet of such religious sensibilities and concerns as Deane.

In the current secular culture it is often difficult for someone characterised as a religious poet to be properly appreciated as a poet. The devoutly religious as well as the non- or anti-religious may crush the poetry beneath the religion and both sides fail to see the poetry as poetry. This may be a parable with wider application as people suborn true humanity to some ideology, religious or non-religious. A religion like Deane's, true to the doctrines of creation and incarnation, should be able to resist that temptation.

Lectio naturalis in Manhandling the Deity
The natural world in its beauties and cruelties is read brilliantly and expressed musically in many of Deane's poems, nowhere more concisely and effectively in this volume than in the short poem, 'Runt Bird'. Only the full text can do justice to the beauty and cruelty:

Runt Bird

Today the adult birds
were inveigling the young from their nest;
come on in, they were calling, the sky is lovely.
The last, the smallest, came

fluttering downwards like an autumn leaf.
I hold it now forever, small as the human heart,
certainly as scared, and its claws
cling to my manflesh. If I fling it into air

it may soar like brother Icarus for one
glorious moment, or fall
on the hard earth where cat and magpie
will be busy in the rutted slaughtering places

and I must tell myself again that this
is runt bird, incapable,
and that the universe that claims us
thrusts on, beautiful and without compassion.

This moving nature poem occurs in the third main section of the collection and after the equally moving but more hopeful and, in the double sense, graceful 'House Martins'. While 'the adults waltzed and tangoed down the air', the young 'cowled and fledgling monks' will soon 'have fled the nest, a little / groggily, but proud as prelates, and you know again / in the secret place within that house's grace, that everything beyond the rule and filthying of men / is whole, and holy, and unsoiled'.

The ecclesiastical images for the young as 'cowled and fledgling monks' in the nest and 'proud as prelates' on fleeing, reflect Deane's religious mindset and prepare the reader for the secret place of grace and everything that is 'whole, and holy, and unsoiled'.

Deane's nature poems here and elsewhere retain their own natural integrity and beauty while reflecting religious sensitivities, whether implicitly as in 'Runt Bird', 'I hold it now forever' or explicitly in 'House Martins' and in the neighbouring poem, 'The Wild Meadow', 'of our universe marvellously wrought'. These and other nature poems, such as the final 'Canticle', reflect what might be called the *lectio naturalis* of the poet, his reading of nature which in all its ambiguity retains for the attentive poet as reader and listener intimations of nature's divine origin and destiny. '(A) night wind mistles through the poplar leaves/and all the noise of the universe stills/to an oboe hum, the given note of a perfect/music'. ('Canticle') As the music of the universe inhabits the poet and finds fresh expression in the poem, reader and listener are offered the two-fold gift of the poem in itself and as new entrance to the natural world it captures. The adult house martins 'who waltzed and tangoed down the air,/each one/a muscle perfected into flight' can never look the same again because the reader/observer can never be the same again. The *lectio naturalis* of the poet, become the *lectio humana* of the reader, involves a conversion process which parallels the poet's own and does not necessarily stop at the human and natural phenomena if poet and reader are sufficiently alert to 'the wild meadow of our universe marvellously wrought', that miracle of creation.

Lectio humana

In his 'human' poems, if one may describe them as such, Deane reveals the extraordinary beauty in the ordinary round of the 'egg-woman' in 'Elliptic', 'generous/with the flesh-browns, the buttermilk-whites/her movements always/close to repose, like the imperceptible/elliptical motion/of the spheres'. But that ordinary and extraordinary were never far from the harshness of 'her space/poverty, and her time/labour'. And the sons she 'birthed', 'Sons to boys to men, she criedeach time they left to build/Birmingham and Liverpool'. 'Between times she tended/ the graves of the parish, seasoning/loss with flowers, sheening –/with her dank sleeve, her chicken-wing/dusters – the incised names who had migrated/to eternity'.

The emigration patterns of his native Achill have given Deane a keen sense of the generations lost, particularly to the West of Ireland. 'The Emigrants' recalls his boyhood memories as in the early morning 'the creaking ... cart' brought emigrants and families to the bus of departure as he heard 'the urgent, hushed, voices,/ nervous shiftings against the dark; ... then those awkward gestures and voices,/ embarrassed kisses and knobbled words/ like sand ramparts against a rising tide,/ how the hurt was held back, the way/ you hold your palm to your side/ to contain the suffering'.

Not all of human life even in Achill was so sad. The joy in

fishing and living, the very frenzied joy of all living comes
through as father and son drifted in 'a small row-boat on Keel
Lake ... till suddenly mayfly were everywhere,/ small water-
coloured shapes like tissue,/ sweet as the host to trout and – by
Jove!/ he whispered, old man astounded again/ at the frenzy
that is in all living'. ('Frenzy')

And not all human sadness is in the countryside. 'In a Shop
Window' is such a compressed account of Deane's capacity to be
invaded by the suffering other and to recognise his own failure
and that of the comfortable class to respond adequately that it is,
like 'Runt Bird', worth quoting in full. Indeed as with 'Runt
Bird' in the *lectio naturalis* section, it may provide the best illustration of Deane's *lectio humana*.

In a Shop Window

He curls into a city doorway,
his night-home refrigerator packing cases,
his mattress last month's newspapers;

the clattering of footsteps past him has grown less,
chocolate wrappers whip in the wind and a can
dances passionately in the gutter;

shaven-headed and unshaven, he is a gathering
of man-stench and garbage smells;
his eyes are dried out seeds and you look

quickly away. Sometime in the night one hand
will fall heavily out along the pavement, palm
upward to the stars, fingers bent so you can see

the perfect quarter-moons of his fingernails,
the lifeline like a contour map of the sky.
This is the very image of God's abdication,

foolish, unlovable, the sheen on glass
throwing back our appalled faces where we stand,
immersed in self as in lambswool coats, certain

of our place in the world, our destination.

An obvious temptation with a poem like this is to concentrate
on the content and then perhaps paraphrase moralistically in
commentary. It happens frequently in homilies on the Sunday
scripture readings in church. With a poem it is particularly easy

to ignore the music and the imagery in search of meaning or moral. Both meaning and moral might be said to be clear here. However for the reader/listener to take the poem into herself she needs to read and listen again and again, to let the poem not only sing to her but to sing in her so that her capacity to see, listen and share in the condition of the doorway refugee matches that of the poet. That should make commentary superfluous and conversion to action possible. Otherwise we remain immersed in self and our worldly certainties.

There are many other rich examples of Deane's *lectio humana* in this collection. 'Alice's Harbour Bar' tells the moving story of one man's search for solace and courage in 'the sickening/frisson of excitement; to be caulked/in companionable darkness, drink/comforting, the world/shaping itself to manageable forms or face/reproach and silence, the harshest judgment/in her sorrow, in the children's eyes/watching him with barely hidden terror'. And for all that a deeply sympathetic poem about a good if broken man. But the 'image of God's abdication'in shop window beckons towards the more explicitly religious poetry and the poet's version of the *lectio divina*.

Lectio divina

The *Officium* prayer-poems, variations on a theme and psalmlike in form and content, which preface the major sections of this ('Mass') collection, might seem the best introduction to the Deane *lectio divina*. They require little commentary and read beautifully if mournfully. In their 'psalmist misery', with their emphais on the sin and suffering of humanity, they may mislead the reader into thinking that the poet has little time for praise, hope and charity. That this is a mistaken reading of him was already apparent in the nature poems. His is a complex relationship with a broken world spelled out with power and majesty in the long and to some shocking religious poem, echoing real 'shock and awe', entitled 'Between Clay and Cloud'.

It proclaims an Ascension Day affirmation of faith in a 'self-broken' God, whose 'love … spun the universe and its derivatives; that he created man in his own image/self-broken and incomplete'.

'And (I believe) in his only Son,/enigma, the Jesus/word uttered/when he spoke/his impulsive foolishness;/creating power/become love become/ man. A man, like men/broken./ After the measured/ballet of reason we step/on the ice of mystery'.

Human sinfulness looms large but 'sometimes the sun shines silently in/ and the beauty of our confined spaces/ shatters us into praise; sometimes,/ when faith, like a firefly, comes glimmering ...'

'And in the Ghost, the aspiration,/ breath of his utterance,/ bolero of winds on the wild meadow, frisson of wisdom along the spine'.

He concludes: 'O broken God be with us always,/ now, and at the end of time.'

His conclusion to another major poem, 'The Wild Meadow', referred to earlier as nature poem but like so many with religious undertones and overtones, takes up again the theme of our brokenness but in a more hopeful mood.

There was one child, East Timor, our time, who fled
terror through the night, who fell and died,
her body splayed where even her doll lay spread

in cruciform shape. Our lives are fragile as the thyme
and celandine, all of us lacking wholeness in our days:
cormorants, militias, God. Attempt the ordering of rhyme.

Attend, be guardian. Love, and offer praise.

The very image of God's abdication in suffering humanity and in a universe without compassion expresses how far the poet is inhabited by breaking humanity and a broken world. Few Irish poets capture the pain so vividly or so beautifully. None recasts it in the cruciform shape that is prelude to resurrection, in the human song that is prelude to praise and prayer. Deane relocates our agony and that of Christ in 'the wild meadow of our universe marvellously wrought'. Mary Pieta and Mary Magdalen are companions on the *via dolorosa* that began with 'His coming so still/ To his mother's bower' and concluded for the drifting woman, with her skirt hiked up, only to be surprised that 'she'd be the one to knock first on the tomb's door'.

As in the beautiful cover, with its reproduction of Tony O' Malley's 1964 Good Friday painting, rumours and glimpses of resurrection abound. And all this summarised in the final poem, 'Canticle', as 'all the noise of the universe stills/ to an oboe hum, the given note of a perfect/ music'. And above 'there is a vast sky wholly dedicated/ to the stars and you know, with certainty,/ that all the dead are out, up there, in one/ holiday flotilla, and

that they celebrate/the fact of a red gate and a yellow moon/
that tunes their instruments with you to the symphony.'

In the Deane office of readings it would be right and proper
to add the categories of *musica naturalis et humana* to that of *lectio
naturalis et humana* in preparation for *musica et lectio divina* accessible to us even now in this 'wild meadow of the universe'.

CHAPTER SIXTEEN

Birds of Contemplation

I. M. Tony O'Malley

In so far as there is a distinction between meditation and contemplation, and not everyone would agree that there is or if there is how it is made, this essay understands meditation as an activity of the human agent and contemplation as a passivity where these words are taken more in a Teilhardian sense. In this sense, there is an element of receptivity or passivity in meditation and an element of activity or creativity in contemplation. Indeed meditation which begins in mental activity focusing on some 'topic', God, human person, event, landscape, object, etc., may lead to contemplation in which the agent surrenders to, is taken over by the presence and power of the 'topic'. The meditating subject is then transformed into the contemplating subject who is no longer self-consciously seeking to explore or understand the 'topic'. Her consciousness has become possessed by the particular 'topic' which is now operating spontaneously from within the subject, as it were. It is with this rather crude understanding that the writer began to approach poems and other works of art, first and very clearly as objects of meditation, only to find that they at least occasionally took him over in what he began to regard as a contemplative experience. In reflecting on this in turn, he began to consider how far the artist might have moved along a similar if deeper, more personal and more sensitive journey. In a further move, how far such moves by artist or reader/observer might relate to religious contemplation and its mature sister mystical prayer, and indeed how far these 'secular' moves could prepare one for the further reaches of prayer.

In an earlier publication, an exercise entitled 'Praying These Poems (*The Small Hours of Belief,* Dublin, 1990), focused as much or more on the theme as on the form of the poem, although its poetic form fuelled and shaped the reader's meditative and prayerful energies. Other art forms and objects offered similar occasions for meditation and prayer. All this naturally prompted more serious reflection on the workings of the artist in producing her work. The creative activity of the artist, in so far as the outsider could understand it, did seem to involve receptivity as well as activity. Ideas came to her, topics took her over, even individual words and lines, brush strokes and subtle colours might come unbidden although the necessary active response could be long and arduous and at times frustrating and even futile, with the work abandoned. A parable of many people's prayer lives. A more detailed analysis of artistic activity and receptivity/passivity, but which far exceeds the limits of this essay, is discussed elsewhere in this book. Here the focus is on individual works and their possibilities as prayer-sources without violation of their artistic integrity.

In recent decades there has been an increasing interaction between artists and art-works of different genres. Paul Durcan and R. S. Thomas have been particularly notable in relating poetry and painting, and the Australian poet Peter Steele SJ has just produced a very fine volume of poems (*Plenty: Art into Poetry*, Melbourne, 2003), inspired by a range of paintings, sculptures and photographs from the fifteenth to the twentieth century and from medieval Europe through modern Australia to Japan. Not all of these, art-works or related poems, have religious motifs but they clearly have something of a shared *spiritus, inspiratio*, spirituality and enthusiasm, in the sense of taking us beyond ourselves. In these 'ekphrastic' poems, as Steele calls them, 'A poet, however zestfully she may respond to a painting or a sculpture, will do no service unless the medium as well as the seen work of art, is brought into celebration' … '(P)oets are mainly on the trace of the Human, that familiar, curious, and largely mysterious creature' … 'Good poetry tries to come clean about the beautiful and the terrible …' And he recognises the influence of Chesterton not as Christian apologist but 'for his unflagging enthusiasm for what need not have been but is, the tipped horn of plenty'. Although Steele's particular poems and paintings will not figure here, the work itself, his reflections in the afterword from which the quotations have come and his recent collection of homilies (*Bread for the Journey*, Victoria, 2002), confirmed an earlier intention to meditate on works of art in their own right and in relation to artistic work in another genre which might enrich the meditation even to the point of contemplation and (dare one say it?) to the point of contemplative prayer.

Birdwatcher artists

Some very good friends are regular birdwatchers who delight in reporting their sightings. Many of us have to be content with watching activity about the bird-feeder and the occasional encounter of singles or flocks on country walks. But birds in song, in plumage and in flight signal the soaring ambitions of the Icarus soul in many and as such have attracted the close observation and creative vision of artists. Shelley's nightingale, like Yeats' swans, have nourished the imagination of schoolchildren and adults. Like so many successful artworks they send the reader or observer back to the originating object with a fresh sensitivity and enriched appreciation of the bird of nature. What captures the artist's attention frequently appeals to the religious imagination as well. Those messengers of God in the Jewish and Christian scriptures known as angels were later to be depicted as winged choristers by writers, painters, sculptors and musicians and so entered and indeed dominated the popular religious imagination. More significantly, God's Spirit herself, the third person of the Trinity-God, was imaged as dove by Christian artists and believers. Against the artistic and religious background so sketchily presented, a personal meditation on related artistic treatments of birds by diverse modern artists is attempted here.

The Windhover

Without some minimal admiration for and enjoyment of real birds, a concentration in Yeats' terms on the painted (or verbal) images would be almost certainly unfruitful artistically (or religiously). The poet Gerard Manley Hopkins and the painter Tony O'Malley, whose poem and painting entitled 'The Windhover' both provide profound bases for meditation and even contemplation, were both keen observers and lovers of nature and of birds as many of their other works and comments confirm. In such serious works of art one may detect a process of observation/meditation which moves to transformation in and through the emotional imagination into the particular artistic expression. All this may happen very quickly, even instantly or quite slowly depending on the particular artist, theme, medium, mood, creative energy, etc etc. In his insightful account of the composition of a particular poem of his own (*Dublin Review* n8, Autumn 2002, pp115-126) Seamus Heaney uses a model devel-

oped by Jacques Maritain to describe 'Creative Intuition in Art
and Poetry', that of 'poetic sense or inner melody related to the
original experience including observation/meditation which
moves into action or theme and issues in the actual writing or
painting, number or harmonic expansion', in Maritain's terms.
What on the basis of Heaney, his sources in Wordsworth,
Maritain and others, and above all his own experience of writing, emerges is some sense of how the transformation is
achieved and how it is given; how the artist is prompted to work
and then is taken over and beyond into the finished poem or
painting. In the more naïve and crude images of the non-artist,
the artist's attention to the original material or object with its
artistic potential develops to the point where the object enters
the artist's self, inhabits her, makes its music in her and becomes
her personal song, her *alter ego* in writing or painting or sculpture.

The notorious density and difficulty of Hopkins' sonnet 'The
Windhover', dedicated to Christ Our Lord, demands knowledge,
attention and perseverance from the reader-interpreter of a
quite unusual kind. In this exercise some of the knottier difficulties and controversies may be laid aside in favour of 'this right-
ness of the thing in the ear [which] is in the end what poetry is all
about'. (Heaney, op. cit., p 121.) Hopkins himself said that his
poems should always be read aloud as it was the music which
matters. He defended his more difficult poems in particular, to
Robert Bridges and other friends, on this musical ground.

The Windhover
To Christ our Lord

I caught this morning morning's minion, king-
dom of daylight's dauphin, dapple-dawn-drawn Falcon, in
     his riding
Of the rolling level underneath him steady air, and striding
High there, how he rung upon the rein of a wimpling wing
In his ecstasy! then off, off forth on swing,
As a skate's heel sweeps smooth on a bow-bend: the hurl and
     gliding
Rebuffed the big wind. My heart in hiding
Stirred for a bird – the achieve of, the mastery of the thing.

Brute beauty and valour and act, oh, air, pride, plume, here
Buckle! AND the fire that breaks from thee then, a billion

Times told lovelier, more dangerous, O my chevalier!
No wonder of it: sheer plod makes plough down sillion
Shine, and blue-bleak embers, ah my dear,
Fall, gall themselves, and gash gold-vermilion.

The octet has all the sweep of the poet's own ecstasy as he reflects on his observation and experience of the bird in early
morning flight. A nature poet of the highest rank, he allows himself to be inhabited and transformed by 'the achieve of, the mastery of the thing' and the alliterative compound words, 'dapple-
dawn-drawn falcon', internal and regular rhymes, what he calls
his 'sprung rhythm', all combine to reach the climactic music of
that final one and a half lines.

My heart in hiding
Stirred for a bird – the achieve of, the mastery of the thing!

The nature mysticism which these eight lines capture could
not stop there for Hopkins. For the reader the lines may move
beyond delight in bird and verse to transfiguring the reader
also, reshaping her from within in some limited analogy of the
poet's inspired condition. Meditation may lead to contemplation in which the initiative lies with the bird, the poet and the
poem rather than with the surrendering reader.

Hopkins as the surrendering writer could not and did not
stop there. His powerful incarnational vision of creation itself
was already evident in the dedication of this poem. And the
vision demanded greater explicitation, even if the language is
still oblique, obscure, perhaps disputable but never unmusical.
However one interprets individual words and phrases the tran-
sition (or should it be transformation?) from bird to Christ works
majestically. The controverted 'Buckle!' of armour or breakdown impels poet and reader into a world of fire, holy fire, both
dangerous and beautiful, breaking from Hopkins' very own
'chevalier', 'Christ our Lord'.

Yet one must not look to such signs and wonders when the
'sheer plod' of daily drudgery has its transforming and 'blue-
bleak embers' 'gash gold-vermilion', The gold of the Risen
Christ carries the vermilion of his passion. In these last three

lines the ordinariness and beauty of nature, as 'plough down sillion shine(s)', give way to the glory of resurrection but only as
they 'Fall [and] gall themselves'. The pain and the ecstasy of divine and human creation are united in a poetic and mystical
vision. At least for one reader they are. Surrendering in this
fashion to the whole poem, even momentarily, seems akin to the
being ravished of which the mystics speak. Hopkins'
Windhover-made-poem-made-Christ is then truly a bird of contemplation.

Tony O' Malley, the distinguished Irish painter who died in
2003, was an admiring reader of Hopkins' poetry and felt a certain kinship with him in musical interests as well as in experi-
mental artistic techniques. In some paintings O'Malley's engagement with music was signaled by tiny birds or tiny musical
notations integrated into the work. Frequently presented as a
purely abstract painter, O'Malley like Hopkins was very attentive to nature and to the birds which he frequently painted on a
large scale. However, he believed in getting to the inner skin of
reality. He even borrowed Hopkins' word 'inscape' to describe
something like the inner depth or space of a painting. In the
homily at his funeral in January 2003, priest-poet Pat O'Brien described him as a contemplative painter. During the funeral-ser-
vice Seamus Heaney introduced and read Hopkins' 'The
Windhover'. O'Malley had at least one painting with that in the
title and had quite a number involving hawks as his main
theme. As bases for meditation or contemplation, painting offers
very different challenges from poetry, at least to this viewer.
With that in mind it may be more valuable to consider one of
O'Malley's windhover/hawk paintings.

These paintings are early in his sojourn at St Ives, Cornwall
and in his preoccupation with the dark, winter, Good Friday
side of life. In his 1963 *The Windhover – He Searches Winter*, the
contrast with the exuberance of Hopkins' opening octet could
hardly be greater. The focused prey-seeking right eye which
dominates the picture prepares the swoop not 'As a skate's heel
sweeps smooth on a bow-bend' but more as an avenging angel
seeking its prey. Yet the angel-wing shapes of the eyes and the
warmer colouring of the surrounds with the indeterminate figures within the right eye, of which one however appears menac-
ing, and the more friendly figures in the top right-hand corner,
including a typical tiny O'Malley self-portrait, qualify the initial

impressions of simple cruelty. It may be that for O'Malley, by temperament a countryman, the 'inscape' of this Windhover embodied the beauty-cruelty of nature, as his Good Friday paintings emphasised human beauty-cruelty with a sense of the creativity and beauty which art and, at its best, the Christian story involved.

Perhaps some of O'Malley's later and lighter paintings are more obviously beautiful and more immediately uplifting. Yet *The Windhover – He Searches Winter* as transformed by the painter, and it may be as transforming him, draws the viewer in eventually through meditation to contemplation of natural and painterly wonder, that carries at least the possibility of being possessed not only by the inscape and spirit of the painting but by the inscape and the spirit of the creating, incarnate and suffering God.

St Kevin and the Blackbird

Seamus Heaney and Imogen Stuart are two of Ireland's most significant living artists. As Nobel Laureate Heaney has attracted so much critical attention that the amateur, particularly the amateur interested in prayer, must be very wary. As a protective measure one might argue that everybody interested or, as the phrase goes, into prayer, is by definition an amateur, both in the original sense of a lover of the practice and in the usual sense today of being a non-professional, aware that s/he is starting over and over again. That does not rule out progress in prayer or the possibility of developing and teaching methods of prayer. But whoever believes he has mastered prayer or even its techniques is likely to be deluding himself. Maybe something similar would be said by serious artists about their own work

That both Heaney and Stuart should independently address in their different media the old Irish legend of St Kevin and the Blackbird is not that surprising. It is one of the most engaging stories in the lives of the Irish saints, combining two of the great characteristics of early Irish Christianity, love of nature and personal, physical asceticism. The narrative is so clear from Heaney that there is no need for a prosaic account.

St Kevin and the Blackbird

And then there was St Kevin and the blackbird.
The saint is kneeling, arms stretched out, inside
His cell, but the cell is narrow, so

One turned up palm is out the window,
Stiff as a crossbeam, when a blackbird lands
And lays in it and settles down to nest.

Kevin feels the warm eggs, the small breast, the tucked
Neat head and claws and, finding himself linked
Into the network of eternal life,

Is moved to pity: now he must hold his hand
Like a branch out in the sun and rain for weeks
Until the young are hatched and fledged and flown.

And since the whole thing's imagined anyhow,
Imagine being Kevin. Which is he?
Self-forgetful or in agony all the time

From the neck on out down through his hurting forearms?
Are his fingers sleeping? Does he feel his knees?
Or has the shut-eyed blank of underearth

Crept up through him? Is there distance in his head?
Alone and mirrored clear in love's deep river,
'To labour and not to seek reward', he prays,

A prayer his body makes entirely
For he has forgotten self, forgotten bird
And on the riverbank forgotten the river's name.

In the first four stanzas Heaney gives his vivid, musical and moving account of the legend. The detail of the picture he paints in simple exact language reveals how far the story and its protagonists have entered into his own consciousness and seek their proper poetic expression. To adapt his own phrase, the poem already has its 'own legs'. For the reader also St Kevin kneeling in his cell with 'arms stretched out' and 'One turned up palm … out the window' is capturing him, as the blackbird landing and nesting in Kevin's outstretched palm captures the saint, linking him 'Into the network of eternal life'. Despite the resonance of that last phrase these first stanzas speak more of nature's hold on saint, poet and reader, rather like the Hopkins octet. Yet the story, as Heaney tells it through the form and language he uses, moves the reader to a first surrender to the beauty and wonder of it.

The further shift and surrender in Heaney's final four stanzas are marked by the deprecating opening line, 'And since the whole thing's imagined anyhow', which leads into the identification with Kevin rather than the legend. 'Imagine being Kevin.' The following stanzas, as they follow Kevin's mental and physical states, the self-forgetfulness or the agony in neck, forearms, sleeping fingers, knees to the stage of loving prayer.

Alone and mirrored clear in love's deep river, / 'To labour and not to seek reward', he prays'.

And then to the stage of total prayer where body, mind and soul are at once united and obliterated, not even the name of love remaining.

'A prayer his body makes entirely, / For he has forgotten self, forgotten bird / And on the riverbank forgotten the river's name.'

One could find in Eckhardt or John of the Cross or a dozen other mystics something of the state Heaney 'imagines' for Kevin or at least what one reader imagines Heaney imagining into that final stanza. If great art derives from fruitful imaginings which take the artist through the labour pains of creation into the gift of poem or picture, it is gift for artist as well as reader / viewer. A gift best accepted and enjoyed in contemplation which stands at the threshold of Kevin imagined in his total prayer .

Imogen Stuart resists the title of religious artist although in a life-time's sculpting she has dealt with many explicitly religious subjects from Stations of the Cross to Madonna with Child to a wide range of saints, Irish and European. She rightly treasures the description of her work as spiritual irrespective of its explicit theme, a point fully illustrated by her delightful *The Fiddler of Dooney and Children*, referring to Yeats' lovely ballad-poem, which stands at the Stillorgan Shopping Centre, Dublin. However, her interest in and knowledge of the early Irish Christian tradition led her to produce, among other works, a number of studies of St Kevin and the Blackbird of varying sizes in wood and bronze .

The one chosen here is in pitch-pine and of medium size and very similar in construction to Heaney's version of the story. Because the writer also had the opportunity to view it a couple of times at close quarters, and even to touch and handle it, it seemed the best choice for the present exercise.

The first impression or impact of this Stuart piece is of compression, the compression of the life of bird and saint and their legendary interaction into the compact cell of wood. The second impression is that of power, due no doubt in part to the power of the pitch-pine itself, a strong wood and very difficult to carve but also to the features of saint and bird. Yet for all their strength and power they are very delicate on eye and hand. Finally there is the serenity as if the bird had the perfect nest and home and Kevin, 'Linked into the network of eternal life' had moved by now to the 'prayer his body makes entirely'.

Drawing on the Heaney lines is not meant to suggest any direct mutual influence. Stuart has been working on this theme at least since 1966 (well before Heaney's poem), when she did one of her most elaborate and beautiful versions of it in Spanish Chestnut. Both artists had lived in Wicklow and no doubt fallen under the spell of Glendalough and the spirit of St Kevin. For the non-artist trying to come to verbal terms with the work of a non-verbal artist, the words of a verbal artist dealing with the same theme can be helpful. However, it is the visual and tactile impact which persists and persistently resists adequate verbal expression. And then one imagines being Imogen and the impact of the story on her and her early sense of how it might be expressed in wood or bronze. And then her being drawn into the labour of carving, her gradual uncovering of the secret of her vision in the wood, her surrender to the gift of her own creation. And then that gift summoning us to creative surrender to the gratuitous wonder and beauty of it as it opens us to the wonder and beauty of the whole of creation and the transforming presence of the ultimate creator.

In laboured pursuit of natural or artistic birds and their settings, this Christian meditator is not seeking to use bird or art object as a means simply to reach some religious or prayerful end. It is in the wonder at and increasing enjoyment of the bird in the bush as well as the bird in poem, painting or carving that he lays himself open to what the creative process and product may eventually bring. In religious and Christian terms that may be sometimes experienced and named as the Creator God. So natural and artistic 'contemplation', if recognised and valued in their own right, may prompt religious contemplation of a significant kind.

CHAPTER SEVENTEEN

Faith and the Artist:
Celebrating Pietro Parigi (1892-1992)

One of the great human and artistic characteristics of Pietro Parigi, if I correctly understand what his friends and critics have to say about him, was his humility. I trust that he will be generous in sharing it this day. I come before you as a theologian, somebody, as a friend said, who is liable to make the most concrete of events from incarnation to crucifixion, inaccessibly abstract. I am thus far removed from the loving strokes and incisions of an artist such as Parigi. And I am Irish, who for all our European pretensions, has only very recently encountered the work of this remarkable artist. So any humility Pietro has to spare, I need in abundance.

In that mood I will toil mainly at my own trade, theology, trying to make some sense of artists and art in the context of the Jewish and Christian traditions of faith in a Creator and Redeemer God. The title assigned to me speaks of a faith living in that mysterious region 'between human wonder and divine attraction'. I would like to explore that region by relating the creating and redeeming/reconciling actions of the God of Jesus Christ to the creating and, as I think, also redeeming actions of various kinds of artists and craft-workers. You may be already rather puzzled by my combining words and concepts which would seem better dealt with separately. I hope, however, that even in this short lecture the close connections suggested between divine creating and human creating, between creating, reconciling and redeeming in both divine and human spheres, and that between art and craft, will appear to have been justified.

For the theologian, the creative work of God has to be expressed however inadequately in the words, images and concepts of human creativity. While every authentic human word and deed, even the simplest sentence, may be said to have a creative element, the creative words and works of artists are the more illuminating here.

These, and the process by which they come to be, are also more obscure to non-artists such as theologians who have to depend on the witness of the artists themselves as well as on the theologians' own capacity to enter sympathetically and analytically into the artistic productions and their genesis.

Human wonder at the world has sought expression in myriad ways over the millennia. At its most intense and profound such wonder found expression in religion, in worship, in recognising the worth-ship and power of the originator(s) and sustainer(s), the god(s) responsible for these wonders. In the Hebrew and Christian traditions the one and only true God is the immediate creator and sustainer of the cosmos, of the earth and of its peoples in all their complex beauty. This beauty of the heavens and the earth showed forth the glory and beauty of God while human beings were created in the very image of God. The human authors of the Hebrew and Christian scriptures were frequently inspired to hymn these wonders and beauty in the finest poetry. Poetic passages from Genesis to Isaiah, to the Psalms and the Song of Songs, from the Prologue of John's gospel to Paul's Letter to the Colossians reveal the human creativity of praise and wonder in response to the divine creativity revealed in God's world and Word, in the accounts of creation and salvation. What Marc Chagall has called 'the greatest work of art in the world', the Bible, has for almost two thousand years inspired in turn some of the greatest literature, music, painting, sculpture and architecture humanity has ever known, expressing in their different ways that humanity's wonder at the God of the Hebrews and of Jesus Christ, and simultaneously raising human hearts and minds to the beauty and majesty of God. In a manner parallel to, if distinct from the great saints, many great artists have opened us up to the attraction of our God.

In the more secular culture of the Western world over the last two centuries, explicitly sacred art using religious themes has diminished if not quite disappeared. Chagall was one of the major opponents of this drift, asking: 'Is there not a foundation for art other than that offered by decorative art which exists only to please, or by the art of experience, and by that pitiless art whose purpose is to shock us?' (He could have been anticipating for example the tasteless 'Brit Art' of Damien Hirst and Tracy Emin and others in the 1990s). In a different but related argument the cultural critic, George Steiner, in his volume, *Real Presences*, invests all great works of art with a presence that is not reducible to words on the page or lines and colours and shapes on the canvas, although these are clearly the medium of the richer and potentially transforming presence. A thought that might echo some other sentiments of Chagall from the passage quoted earlier: 'If the theoretical and scientific sources of art and life of which I have spoken earlier could be subordinated to love, their results might become valid and more just. In connection with art I have often spoken of the colour which is love.'

For the believer and the theologian, the artistic route to the attraction and presence of God focuses first of all on the object produced by the artist – the painting, the music, the poem. Its beauty draws reader or listener into a new world which, if the power of the product and sensibility of reader/viewer connect effectively, has elements of the 'new creation' envisaged by St Paul. A certain conversion to the beautiful in its spiritual as well as its bodily dimensions may be experienced, with perhaps the call of English Jesuit poet, Gerard Manley Hopkins, ultimately to be heard: 'Give beauty back, give beauty back to God.' Few modern poets combined such beauty of form with such at once celebratory and agonising sense of the presence of God in nature, people and historical events such as the wreck of the German ship the Deutschland. It sank off the coast of Britain in 1879 and, along with the crew and passengers, five German Franciscan nuns perished who had been expelled from

Germany under the new Falk laws of religious persecution. Acting on the suggestion of his superior, Hopkins broke his self-imposed poetic silence to write this major poem in which human wonder and divine attraction are combined in the most powerful and transforming ways. Pietri's contribution to Margherita Guidacci's powerful poem, *l'orologio di bologna*, on the 1980 outrage at Bologna railway station, reflects a similar artistic concern with great human tragedies.

For the believer and theologian, the magnificent productions of a Hopkins or Chagall, of Michelangelo, Bach or Dante offer more than enough nourishment for faith, and indeed hope and love, as they allow these works to inhabit them and lead them on to give beauty back to God. The process of human creation by artists provides further illumination for Christian faith and divine attraction. And one of the values of this approach is that the unartistic among us can appreciate from within, as it were, something of the human creative process. In the very act of writing or speaking a sentence we share some of the difficulty and the joy of a proper literary artist. Poor craftworkers we may be in this as in other areas of activity but the making of a sentence and of sense to our neighbour is from another perspective a genuine creative achievement which, on reflection, gives us an insight not only into procedures of the human artist, major or minor, but into procedures and achievements of the divine artist. The wonder evoked at our own completed sentence will not we hope delude us into thinking of ourselves as artists. Craftspeople at best we share in a very humble way in the great human and divine creative enterprise. That is also a significant element of our Christian faith, that we be able to interpret ourselves as co-workers of the Creating and of the Redeeming/ Reconciling God.

The creative work of the human artist might be analysed in terms of how far the work is simply a question of human struggle and achievement and how far it is inspiration and gift. Many artists acknowledge it as both. The major American poet Richard Wilbur has often spoken of poems as happening to him or at least of the theme/title/first lines coming to him out of the blue, as gift or inspiration. Other poets, composers and painters record similar experiences. Leading Irish painter, Tony O' Malley (1913-2003), has spoken of picking up a piece of driftwood and letting it lead him on into the shapes and colours which emerge as a new expression of beauty. More deliberately, he set about a new painting every Good Friday on a related theme but waited upon the Spirit for more exact specification which only gradually appears. He has described himself as servant of the work which is basically gift. In such testimony we find real parallels to the graces and gifts, the struggles and achievements of saints and sinners. The beauty-making of the artist and the holy-making of the believer, however inadequately in either case, reflect the creative and sanctifying work of God.

They also reflect God's redeeming and reconciling work which so preoccupied St Paul. In his Second Letter to the Corinthians, Paul describes God as reconciling the world to himself in Christ and speaks of us Christians as his ambassadors of reconciliation. The holy-making is then a task of redeeming and reconciling in a world disfigured by sin. So is the beauty-making in a world also disfigured by ugliness. The poet redeems the language, the painter reconciles in line and colour the destructiveness all about us. Sometimes of course he must do that by revealing the truth and depth of that ugliness just as Christ did on the cross. In doing so, the artist is also performing a redeeming and reconciling task.

Here it would be useful to discuss the traditional difficulty of the hubris of art and of the artist. The creative power and thrust of some artists may lead them into the age-old human temptation of aspiring to equality with God. However this divine ambition may express itself in social and family behaviour, and it has done so very destructively in the lives of artists as of others, the real artists seem to have been very humble before their work. Pietro Parigi, as I mentioned at the outset, was personally a very humble man and I have no doubt that in his artistic pursuits, modesty before the materials, the craft and skills he developed and the beautiful work he produced was an enduring feature. One could almost infer such modesty from his choice of material, of particular art-form in xilografia, for which we have no such beautiful word in English. His Franciscan engagement in so much of his work and his attention to the sacred and Christian animal, the donkey (another echo of Chagall), suggest a very strong Christian foundation to his work. And what has been called the *violenza armoniosa, bianco e nero* reveals the depths of our graceful-sinful world.

Let me close with a poem from an Irish contemporary of Parigi, who died however some decades before him. Patrick

Kavanagh came from a poor peasant family and, like Parigi, was basically self-educated. His poetry had much of the sharp contrasts Parigi revealed and also much of Parigi's deep faith. This poem, 'Advent', written in the 1940s, expresses something of the modesty, the penitential discipline and the openness to beauty to which artist and Christian are called.

Advent

We have tested and tasted too much, lover –
Through a chink too wide there comes in no wonder.
But here in the Advent-darkened room
Where the dry black bread and the sugarless tea
Of penance will charm back the luxury
Of a child's soul, we'll return to Doom
The knowledge we stole but could not use.

And the newness that was in every stale thing
When we looked at it as children: the spirit-shocking
Wonder in a black slanting Ulster hill
Or the prophetic astonishment in the tedious talking
Of an old fool will awake for us and bring
You and me to the yard gate to watch the whins
And the bog-holes, cart-tracks, old stables where Time begins.

O after Christmas we'll have no need to go searching
For the difference that sets an old phrase burning –
We'll hear it in the whispered argument of a churning
Or in the streets where the village boys are lurching.
And we'll hear it among simple decent men too
Who barrow dung in gardens under trees,
Wherever life pours ordinary plenty.
Won't we be rich, my love and I, and please
God we shall not ask for reason's payment,
The why of heart-breaking strangeness in dreeping hedges
Nor analyse God's breath in common statement.
We have thrown into the dust-bin the clay-minted wages
Of pleasure, knowledge and the conscious hour –
And Christ comes with a January flower.

CHAPTER EIGHTEEN

Although It Is The Night
A St Patrick's Day Reflection, 2000

Trying to address the contemporary Irish condition in the light of the Irish spiritual tradition is beset with difficulties. Despite the present fashion for things Celtic and spiritual, despite the best-seller achievement of John O'Donohue's *Anam Chara, Spiritual Wisdom from the Celtic World,* that wisdom is not easily accessible or applicable. Indeed some Irish scholars, not all the dry sticks of Yeats' or Kavanagh's imaginations, regard Celtic in this as in other fields as a suspect word, at once too broad and too narrow. Reflecting on St Patrick's legacy on this day and in relation to Ireland now, suggests concentrating on the Irish rather than ambitioning the Celtic. Scholarly and personal limitations are further confining in the search for some light from the tradition on that most obscure period of all, the present.

The celebration of nature in word and ritual seems an essential element of early Irish religion, Christian and pre-Christian. We depend on Christian sources for what may have been pre-Christian attitudes and practices but there is sufficient evidence to indicate a prior sacred attitude to nature and to natural phenomena. This was integrated into Christianity in the doctrine of a creation to which the triune Creator-God was intimately present. The nature poems of the monks and their seeking out of beautiful, if wild and isolated, settings to settle, from Aran to Skellig Michael, confirms their sense of the beauty to be found in creator and creation and for which praise and thanksgiving are always in order.

'The Hermit's Song' (9th century) is a popular example of the monk's 'green' spirituality as it might be termed today: 'I wish, O Son of the living God, O ancient, eternal King, / For a hidden little hut in the wilderness that it may be my dwelling. / An all-grey little lark to be by its side, / A clear pool to wash away sins through the grace of the Holy Spirit. / Quite near, a beautiful wood around it on every side, / To nurse many-voiced birds, hiding it with its shelter ...' (Translation, Kuno Meyer)

'The Breastplate of St Patrick' from the 8th century invokes not only the protection of the tri-personal God and of the heavenly court but also of the natural elements themselves. 'I arise today / Through a mighty strength, the invocation of the Trinity ... / I arise today / Through the strength of heaven: / Light of sun, / Radiance of moon / Splendour of fire, / Speed of lightning ...'

Of themselves or by their essence or nature, as Seán Ó Ríordáin, the great twentieth-century poet might put it, the natural elements praise God. 'Only a fool would fail / To praise God in his might / When the tiny mindless birds / Praise him in their flight.' (8th century, translation Brendan Kennelly) The poetry of the 8th century monk Blathmac is even more daring as he visualises the elements keening the death of Christ and even having to be restrained from destroying his executioners. The last stage in this development may be found in the tenth-century (?) text , *The Ever-renewed Tongue of Philip*, in which the apostle Philip, whose tongue was cut out many times and always renewed, explains to the sages of Israel how the risen Christ is the centre and completion of creation, a scriptural theme also of course.

The unity of Creator and creation, of humanity, nature and grace, of this world and the others, however one expresses it, is powerfully present in early Irish spirituality. To some ancient and modern critics this sometimes smells of heresy, where there is no distinction between Creator and creation (pantheism), or where humanity and nature are sufficient unto themselves without need of God or grace (a form of heresy attributed to the Celtic / British monk, Pelagius). These readings are almost certainly incorrect, although at this level of mystery involving the relation between Creator and creation, so much passes our understanding that all our words are inadequate.

The Irish poetic and spiritual traditions have never quite lost this sense of affinity with nature. Today the embryonic 'green' movement, with its many women feminist activists, has reached back to these early traditions. And if some appear to dismiss the Christian element, such spirituality of the earth has the kind of Christian potential which the early Irish Christians discerned and developed. An eco-theologian like Seán McDonagh has grasped the need for systematic theological reflection on our relation to the environment, while John O'Donohue's writings embrace the natural world at a more poetic and prayerful level with remarkable resonance for many people in search of a contemporary spirituality. All this in imaginative transformation of earlier Irish and Christian traditions.

Creation and creativity were happily conjoined in early and medieval Irish Christianity. The recent exhibition at the National Museum of the Sacred Treasures of the Medieval Church, and which originally inspired these reflections, illustrate how the creative gifts of human beings in all the arts reflect the creative spirit which Christians identify with God and so continue the praise of that creative spirit which birds in their flight already announce. Irish artists, across all the boundaries, verbal and visual, musical and plastic, elitist and popular, release much of the spiritual energy of contemporary Ireland as ancient and medieval artists did. The Christian dimension of artists' work today is less transparent than that of many of their predecessors, but it remains genuinely spiritual work from which servants of the Spirit of Christ have much to learn.

Two recent articles in *The Irish Times* exposed the gulf today between the Christian spiritual leader and the artistic spiritual leader. In an article on the problems and opportunities facing the Catholic Church in Ireland and published February 21, Cardinal Desmond Connell properly stressed the centrality of the person of Christ for a healthy human individual and society. This message should be mediated to all through the church, the sacrament, effective sign of a whole and holy human community. However, little or no reference was made to the complex Irish society in which we now live, to a spiritual leader's need to understand the strengths and weaknesses of that society, to the entry points into that society for people preaching the good news of Jesus Christ or to the language they need to learn. In these respects, contemporary Irish Christian leaders may have much to learn from their predecessors in the early church who seemed to baptise and integrate so freely the cultural practices and achievements of their time. In an unrelated article published a few days later, February 26, the painter Hughie O'Donoghue discussed the proposal for a statue of Christ in central Dublin as a millennium memorial. As the painter of a monumental series of paintings of the passion of Christ, still looking for a permanent home in Ireland, he might be expected to be sympathetic to the proposal. His final judgement was not entirely negative but he questioned the possibility of a Christ figure adequately representing in public the present confused and divided religious

views of the Ireland of today. This point is certainly open to debate. His more serious concern was that it should be first of all a
fine piece of artwork which would then embody its own spiritual
values. The distance between these two positions and the dialogue they require might well be accomodated by a greater
awareness of the Patrician legacy we celebrate today.

For all the delight in nature and homeland which the early
Irish Christians displayed, this was apparently contradicted by
two other notable aspects of their spirituality, penance and pilgrimage even into exile. The renouncing of the comforts of this
life under a severe monastic rule and the painful leaving of
home and kinsfolk by Columba and Columbanus, among count-
less others, in order to preach the gospel anew, was a clear indic-
ation of the importance attached to asceticism and self-surrender by people who recognised fully the joys of nature. The ascetical practices were first of all a training in focusing on the central features of life, above all the relationship with the Creator-
God without whom creation made no sense. Saint Paul used this
athletic image of the Christian life and all human achievement is
based on disciplined application. Few people know better than
great artists how much attentive, even ascetical application goes
into their work, and yet as Irish painter Tony O'Malley has re-
marked, the created work comes as gift in the end. (No heretical
Pelagianism there.) For many Irish monks their self-discipline
was not a denial but a preparation of the body for its own glory
in resurrection. Penance and self-mortification involve also of
course reparation for one's own sins and those of others and in
this they are associated with the redemptive sufferings of Christ.
All human suffering, however unmerited, is given some positive
value in relation to Christ's suffering and death and so in relation to resurrection.

Pilgrimage had its penitential side as the two most famous
traditional pilgrimages in Ireland, to Lough Derg and Croagh
Patrick, make clear. Croagh Patrick was certainly a pre-Christian
holy place. In John O'Donohue's modern phraseology, mountains are gestures of transcendence. Pilgrimage was above all a
conversion process, as the scholarly work of Victor and Edith
Turner has shown. One leaves behind the life in which one has
become entrapped to seek a new vision and a new lifestyle. For
some of the Irish voyagers, pre-Christian as well as Christian,
the quest was for Hy Brasil, Tír na nÓg, Heaven, the New

Creation. The voyages of Bran and of Brendan illustrate these themes wonderfully. In the voyage for Christ *(perigrinatio pro Christo)*, Irish Christians set off into the unknown to bring the gospel to the European lands of the Dark Ages. Emigrants and missionaries from nineteenth and twentieth-century Ireland emulated, often unconsciously, these early monks. In today's Ireland that tradition is renewed in other forms by young Irish people volunteering to work in the developing world. Without engaging in any kind of religious imperialism, the spirituality of these volunteers, their vision, ideals and self-giving energies might be harnessed to a more worthy celebration of Patrick, who returned to the land of his enslavement to preach the gospel of freedom.

An unusual and provocative echo of the Croagh Patrick legend occurred in 1999 when Mayo Artist in Residence, Chris Doris, spent forty days and forty nights on top of the Reek (its local pet-name) from late July to early September. His was indeed a spiritual quest endured in real hardship. As his writing, photographs and paintings made at the time indicate, the mystical element, or the altered consciousness as he might call it, transcends both the hardships undergone and the distractions encountered. Six thousand people climbed the Reek while he was there.

Spirituality is finally about human freedom and fulfilment. For all the extension of choice in so many areas which the new prosperity offers Irish people, and they are not to be simply denied or denigrated, many people feel themselves enslaved in various ways. The Celtic tiger can be a hard taskmaster as the daily commuter knows only too well. Could the legacy of dialogue and integration, which an older spirituality accomplished, provide any kind of model for a new spiritual liberation? At least that is the kind of question one might ask on St Patrick's Day.

For those for whom the question is pointless, because they have no sense of enslavement or darkness, as well as for those who are all too conscious of darkness and are beginning to despair of modern materialist Ireland, a couple of stanzas from a poem by the great Spanish mystic, John of the Cross, as translated by Seamus Heaney, may offer some solace.

How well I know that fountain,
filling, running,
although it is the night.

That eternal fountain hidden away,
I know its haven and its secrecy
although it is the night
…

I am repining for that living fountain.
Within this bread of life I see it plain
although it is the night.

PART FIVE

The Vulnerable Self

CHAPTER NINETEEN

The Risk of Priesthood

It was far from obvious fifty years ago, the risk. At least the seventy-six first-year clerical students who entered Maynooth in 1948 would not have thought in these terms. Not that they were clear about what they wanted or had much idea about what to expect in the years ahead. From a variety of backgrounds and for a mixture of motives, they were prepared to give training for the priesthood a try. About one-third dropped out during the seven years of training, some for health reasons but most by personal choice. It was perhaps fifteen or more years later, almost ten years into their priestly ministry, that they might have begun to understand some of the risks involved. By the early 1970s, priesthood was clearly perceived as a risky business. Many of the already ordained had begun to drop out and new entrants had begun to drop off. The pattern has continued although the correlation between that kind of increasing risk and decreasing numbers is far from clear.

Risk is not a regular ecclesiastical or theological word. It is not a recognised ecclesiastical or theological practice either. Prudence is the word and caution the practice. Indeed the prudence and caution characteristic of so much church leadership and practice may be more responsible for the present demoralisation of priests and the decline in recruitment. Such a judgement moves beyond the immediate concern of the social and cultural risks to priesthood in the present prosperous and (one hopes) peaceful Ireland, which has also been described as a post-Catholic or a post-Christian Ireland. The growing illusion of attaining heaven on earth and the proper refusal to endure hell on earth draw the different constituencies, advantaged and disadvantaged, away from any conventional religious view of eternal salvation beyond this life. The priestly crisis is first of all a faith crisis, for the people from whom the priests must come and to

whom they must go. Inevitably it becomes a faith crisis for some
of the priests themselves. They are not isolated from cultural
trends and the people affected by them, not if they are to be of
any worth as pastors. Potential candidates educated and developed in this increasingly secular climate cannot easily discover
the value and need of priestly service. It is a risky enterprise,
priestly or religious life, which fewer and fewer of the most adventurous of young people ever consider.

Lamenting the social climate may relieve certain ecclesiastical anxieties. It seldom results in creative response. Like the
women of Jerusalem, we might be better advised to weep for
ourselves and for our children (past students at least). Repenting
our own blindness and mistakes may be the only way to the
kind of *metanoia* (conversion) which Jesus demanded for entry to
the kingdom. The risks not taken by bishops, priests and religious, past and present, may prove to have more serious consequences for the survival of church and priesthood than many
aspects of rampant Celtic tigritude.

Risk is an inherent quality of Christian discipleship. Leaving
all things they followed him. Risk is intrinsic to life itself. All important stages in life involve risk, from birth to choice of profession to choice of partner. The risk of faith has additional, less
comprehensible or controllable dimensions as one enters into
engagement with the supreme mystery of life. To fall into the
hands of the living God and to do so knowingly and willingly
can indeed be terrifying. Surrendering to love, absolute love, is
fraught with risk and, for all the moments of intimacy and ecstasy,
which may be few and far between, remains a hazardous and
uncertain adventure. Without that openness to adventure and
risk, faith becomes the lukewarm consolation of the cautious,
neither hot nor cold; the salt losing its savour.

For those addicted to the short-term delights of the consumer
and virtual worlds, the possibility and the risk of God or faith
may never surface. But what of all the thoughtful, committed
and critical people in politics, the professions, the arts as well as
in the less glamorous occupations from bus driver to housewife
or house-husband? Are they unwilling or unable to consider seriously the risk of faith? Clearly some are not. Yet public discussion in Ireland would not suggest much thoughtful consideration of crucial and ultimate issues like the meaning and destiny
of humanity and the world. Polarisation on certain moral issues

in the recent past plays an inhibiting role. So does the religious dimension of the Northern Ireland troubles and of the many internal conflicts around the world from Yugoslavia to Sri Lanka. The absence of theological education from so many third-level institutions for so long, deprived many people of the knowledge and skill which could have made for critical conversation on the risks of faith. But as Pope Paul VI pointed out almost forty years ago, self-styled believers exercise important influence on the unbelief of their contemporaries. In so far as Christian faith is an exciting adventure involving risk, the faith-community and its leaders do not look very adventurous, exciting or risk-taking to most observers, including perhaps candidates who might take on the risk of priesthood.

In his valuable and widely discussed book, *The Changing Face of the Priesthood*, Donald B. Cozzens offers fresh thinking on the crisis in priestly life and in vocations. His insightful use of the Oedipus story as metaphor for priest-bishop and priest-priest relations reveals his strength as a psychologist, while his balanced chapter on gay priests and seminarians deserved better journalistic treatment than even *The Tablet* managed. The book speaks out of and to his American experience but much of it has broader validity. More serious limitations are his rather cursory reference to the wider possibilities of ministry and priesthood with the attendant risks, and his undeveloped discussion of the relation between baptism/confirmation and ministry/priesthood. Despite a sensitive section on intimacy, the heroic celibate male remains the only model of priesthood. Its risks, positive and negative, are not given any theological probing. The face of the priesthood will have to change much more radically if the present challenges are to be met. Theology will have its own role and must take its own risks in that change.

Disciples, ministers and priests
The search for a Christian theology of priesthood has quite serious problems, particularly if you include, as you must, the New Testament. Priesthood, as is well known is used in reference to the one new High Priest, Jesus Christ (Hebrews 4:14) or to the priestly people or disciples in community (1 Peter 2:5 and 8). These are the two poles between which any Christian discussion of priesthood must operate. Too much Christian reflection on priesthood (including that of Cozzens) concentrates on the Jesus

pole with rather implausible remarks about the (male) priest as the only, or at least predominant, icon/symbol of Christ. The romantic reproduction of the head of Christ attributed to Rembrandt on the cover of Cozzens' book confirms this tendency.

The object of this article is not to rehearse old debates but to reroot the risk of Catholic priesthood as we have it today in the risks of discipleship and ministry as witnessed in the New Testament and in the Christian tradition. In a simple theological as well as chronological sense, discipleship precedes ministry, which precedes priesthood. Circularity might image their relationship better than linearity. All the believing and baptised are at once disciples, ministers and priests. As vowed religious or commissioned ministers or ordained priests, their ecclesial identities and tasks may differ from the simply baptised and believing, but it is in that same reality of Jesus Christ that such identities and tasks, with their accompanying risks, are founded and renewed. There is no deeper Christian gift or grace than that of being disciple of Christ, incorporated by faith and baptism into the Body of Christ, the priestly people, the communal servants/ministers of the reign of God. To that foundation all commissioned ministers and all ordained priests must in the company of the faithful continually return for nourishment and renewal. It is the deeper risks of that basic call to a priestly, ministerial discipleship that they must share and overcome.

Disciples in community in formation

Every Christian starts out as a disciple. Given the graces of repentance and perseverance, s/he hopes to die as one. Baptised or ordained, bishop or pope, the first and last call is to live and die a disciple of Jesus Christ. The post-Vatican II difficulties about the identity of the ordained priest might have been less painful and confusing if the prior identity of disciple had been kept more firmly in mind. Indeed the recent decline of episcopal and papal authority might have been much less severe if it had been understood and exercised by disciples with disciples and not in the 'My Lord-ing' gentile style. The fuller integration of bishops and priests into the community of disciples is essential to the recovery of the identity of the priest and the renewal of the authority of the bishop (and the pope). It would also further reduce the risk of those two destructive clerical weaknesses, mitre-ambition and mitre-envy – a diminishing risk at present, given the unhappy situations in which many bishops find themselves.

Disciples originate and grow, are formed in community, a company of friends in one of Jesus' most famous descriptions. The development of such communities is the historic task of the church as a whole although bishops and priests over the centuries have been given or have taken more or less exclusive charge of this development. In the present crisis of church and priesthood the gifts, energies and initiatives of the full community of disciples will be needed. To stimulate and share in these energies, priests (and bishops) will have to take many risks.

In recovering the primacy of baptism and discipleship, the ordained is bound to feel the tension experienced between professional and lay in most walks of life. The demystification of the professions which proceeds in varying degrees in various professions has its own complexities in relation to the ordained priesthood. The sex-abuse scandals intensified in a destructive way a social process that the clergy, like many professionals, were undergoing anyway. That process was, for the clergy, passive and even then mainly negative because they had not positively worked out and embraced their reintegration into the company of disciples. For most priests and many people the aura of superior mystery-man, even magic-man, was too comforting to be readily and affirmatively surrendered. Professionalism is not to be lightly dismissed and there were and are many fine priest-professionals. It is, however, an awkward and often ambiguous term for priests. That they should have the training, skills and commitment to carry out their professional duties of celebrating the liturgy, of preaching and teaching the word of God, of caring pastorally for a range of people in need and of building the local community-church is not open to dispute, even when they inevitably vary in their skills and commitment and dutifulness. Yet as disciples they are primarily people of faith, hope and love for which no training, skill or even professional commitment can substitute. It is the faith, hope and love of their friends and companions in discipleship who will sustain and renew their deeper needs in faith, hope and love. For that to happen they will have to shed the protection of their professionalism as humble fellow-pilgrims with the least ones.

The risk to office and to respect for office, as it is called, is in the Christian context largely phoney. After the example of Jesus, what Christian leader can clothe himself in the protection of office? After the recent clerical scandals, what priest or bishop can demand any more reverence than the least of his fellow Christians and fellow citizens? Joining the community in full solidarity and self-giving service is the only Christian way to earn anew respect for person and office. The equality of discipleship must be enthusiastically embraced and lived by those who would be leaders.

Isolation and superiority surrounding priesthood offered protection also from the risks of friendship and intimacy, from the risk of one's own feelings. This was often encouraged and reinforced in seminary training and left one unprepared for the turbulence of later emotional life. In the community of disciples – the company of friends, as Jesus called it – the risks and the rewards of friendship are everyday occurrences. For the celibate priest the stabilising influence of some intimate friendships in both his personal and ministerial life are essential. They are given thoughtful consideration in Cozzens' recent book. It is in this untidy and sometimes chaotic life that the priest shares the joys and the pains of individual families and parishioners in ways which should enrich his working with them in word and sacrament and pastoral care.

Minister among the ministering
As disciple among the disciples the priest realises afresh that he is always a minister in the midst of a company of ministers, formal and informal, in church, family and society. The priest-minister has much to learn from the ministering of parents, teachers and community workers of all kinds. And he has a great deal to gain from engaging in direct collaborative church ministry with parishioner-disciples. By faith and baptism all disciples are called to minister in Christ's name, to serve one another and the wider world, to announce and promote the transforming reign of God. In a particular parish or local church some will be needed and called to serve that church in specific ways, from ministers of the Eucharist and of the Word in the present very restricted senses, to much fuller involvement and responsibility across a range of ministries now usually left to the priest or simply neglected through lack of time or interest. The effective parish priest operates with a team and like any successful team manager has a well-trained squad who can be called on in emergency or simply in rotation of duty. The priest-minister in his new-found discipleship discovers the ministerial call and quality of his

new-found co-disciples. The disciples discover through their ministry, informal as well as formal, the excitement and the risks of the servant-followers of Jesus.

Servant-followers as leaders
The language of church and theology has never managed entirely satisfactory terms and descriptions for the sacramentally or- dained ministers. This is, as noted already, evident in the New Testament where priesthood and ordination do not appear in the usual contemporary senses. In the wake of Vatican II, as Cozzens among others comments, the emphasis has moved from the cultic priesthood into which I and my classmates were certainly ordained. Leadership in the celebration of the eucharist is still central yet the priest is not the only active participant in that work of the people, liturgy. He can no longer properly speak of 'my Mass' as in 'I will offer my Mass for your inten- tions.' Preaching and teaching the word, together with pastoral care and community building have assumed equal importance with celebration of the sacraments for the ordained leader, how- ever he is called. These three elements in his ministry belong to- gether and, in the broader understanding of Christian ministry now acceptable, may and should be shared appropriately but clearly with non-ordained ministering disciples.

As the leadership of the ordained in its discipleship and serv- ing mode is not a concession to efficiency in organisation but a genuine faith role which has evolved over the centuries and is naturally open to further evolution, so the sharing of the leader's tasks is not a concession to the shortage of ordained ministers but a consequence of the ministerial call of all disciples. Of course priest shortage makes all the more urgent the recognition of the ministries of the baptised and confirmed and their sharing in the more traditionally priestly ministries from preaching to the faith-care of the sick. In passing, one wonders why women with particular gifts have not been encouraged into faith-care of the sick and others, as hospital chaplains and parish visitors, and why those who perform the caring should not be commissioned to celebrate the sacrament of the sick. The parachute visit of the ordained just for the sacrament shows little respect for sacra- ment or sick person.

All at once the risks of shared ministry are uncovered. Can it stop where the bishop or priest now draws the line? The lines are of course still important but as history shows they may be drawn in different places at different times. Without rehashing the arguments about married priests or the readmission of priests who have resigned and are married – matters changeable at the stroke of a pen – and leaving aside the controversial issue of ordaining women priests – a controversy which clearly has not been settled by the stroke of a pen – the church cannot for theological reasons deny or for practical reasons ignore the ministerial potential of all the disciples. Indeed living for the moment with the restrictive practice of accepting only male celibate priests in the Catholic Church of the Western Rite demands a much wider participation in commissioned and non-commissioned ministry by married and single, male and female disciples. The ordination of male deacons will not only contribute little to the rich variety of ministry now needed, it will give further offence to many committed women in the church. The risks of much wider commissioning to ministry and so of much broader sources of human and divine energy must be undertaken with full trust in the Spirit who is always available to the church, but too often ignored.

Vocations go leor?
The declining number of ordained priests and of candidates for ordination should not, theologically speaking, be called a vocations crisis. To do so is to ignore some Christian basics. The primary Christian vocation as elaborated earlier is that to discipleship. That vocation is to be cherished and nurtured in themselves and in others by the ordained as well as by the baptised and the confirmed. The decline in the number and commitment of the disciples would be the real crisis in vocations. It may be already happening in Ireland, although Mass attendance figures and other external criteria are not necessarily the best basis for comparing present and past. Neither are the numbers entering seminaries or religious houses.

The declining numbers entering seminaries and religious houses may indeed be some indicator of a decline in discipleship. That decline may also be attributed, positively to a stronger sense of the primary value of discipleship, or negatively to the obscuring of the adventure of ordination by clerical scandal and lack of leadership. The old recruiting cry of the forties and the fifties, 'Who has a blade for a splendid cause?' sounds pretty hollow today. The splendid causes can seem very foreign in the present clerical world.

Yet even in ecclesial terms it is a time for hope rather than despair. Admittedly hope and despair are more closely connected in human and Christian terms than is usually allowed. The despair may be promoted by the usual 'prophets of doom' but the hope lies in the energy of so many Spirit-filled disciples. Where the energy is, there is the creative spirit. And there is so much energy and creativity in Ireland at present that it would be tragic if disciples who share this energy and can identify it with the Holy Spirit as well as the human spirit were not free to release that energy into the church. The current commercial and industrial enterprise has its own spiritual and creative energy, however much influenced by personal aggrandisement as against the community good. The explosion in artistic energy over the past couple of decades could indeed be displacing previous religious energy but it could also truly nourish a new mode of Christian vitality. The justice-seekers, individual and organised, provide models which disciples of the prophetic Jesus should assist and imitate. In a frighteningly energetic society, the Irish church must endorse and help harness the energy positively or decline into irrelevance. Out of that energy pool in which disciples are naturally immersed will come the new and creative Christian leaders. There is no shortage of Christian vocations, baptised, commissioned or ordained, the shortage is of channels for their energetic realisation. If we need vocations directors they should direct themselves to the broader calls of discipleship and ministry within which authentic leaders of the local Christian community will emerge.

Preparing for priesthood
In the first place, as they are disciples in community any formal training of candidates for the priesthood should be training in discipleship in a community of disciples. If it is in a seminary, as is customary at present, the candidates should share community with other disciples in the course of formation. This formation would have its spiritual, academic and social dimensions which demand careful working out in each different context. Academically candidates and other disciples might share joint study, and if possible degrees, partly in theology and partly in secular subjects. All disciples need further education not only in the

Christian tradition but in the great humanistic and scientific traditions if they are to be adequate witnesses to the creator and redeemer God of Jesus Christ. The spiritual, moral, psychological and social formations may be more difficult to harmonise but they should not be simply separate for the disciplines or for the two groups. Disciples without aspirations to the priestly and religious life have for too long been deprived of any systematic development in these areas. The same might be said of citizens generally whose further education seldom includes any even non-religious development in areas so essential to the health of society.

The second phase should concentrate on ministry and be pursued in a community of disciples who are seeking commissioned as well as ordained ministry. In this context potential candidates for both kinds of ministry, together with their directors, will be able to discern their more exact calling. Academic and professional skills courses, complemented by practical placements carefully supervised, will take their education as disciples and potential ministers into deeper and more challenging areas. The risk of fall-out will inevitably increase but it should be a more informed departure from the prospect of ministry with a much better understanding of the gift and call of discipleship. In the more remote past seminarians often left with a sense of failure, and even in the more recent past without much awareness of their continuing call to discipleship. The spiritual, moral and other aspects of the training programme will focus heavily on ministry as a commissioned service within the community of disciples in promotion of the reign of God.

The final phase of immediate preparation for ordination will theologically focus again on the sacraments, particularly the eucharist and penance (disgracefully underdeveloped in theological and pastoral terms). The theology of Orders as a sacrament of service within the community, and its wider range of ministries, fits naturally into this final phase as the sacraments of baptism and confirmation fit into the first. The theology of the Word and its practical translation in preaching will require much sharper realisation than was necessary earlier. This phase should also include some substantial placement time, as the apprentice is required to prove himself.

This rough sketch of a preparation programme is designed merely to illustrate the more substantial message of returning the ordained priesthood to its rightful place in the community of ministerial disciples. Much more reflection and experimentation are needed before the details of any such programme could be finalised. Meantime there is the duty to assist the ordained and the seminarians who are there with all the risks to which they are exposed.

Priests are the most exposed of disciples. Their failures and wrongdoings are more readily observed and criticised than those of other disciples. Perhaps that is as it should be given the public service they have undertaken and the privileges they enjoyed, at least in the past. They might also have better spiritual resources to deal with criticism and rejection if they have absorbed some central strands of their central message about the teaching, life and death of Jesus Christ. In language not regularly used, the whole story of God and Jesus, of God in Jesus, might be recounted in terms of risk. The often criticised male celibate priests of today, whoever their successors may be, are also at high risk. May the Breastplate of Patrick be our shield.

CHAPTER TWENTY

Letter to Sarah

Dear Sarah,
The letter promised on the occasion of your baptism inevitably came to nothing. A fresh promise to write something on 'The Sources of Spirituality' prompts this further attempt to address your future faith. Topic and title are too daunting for both of us, given the elusiveness of 'spirituality' and the endless possibilities of 'sources'. Ruthless reduction is the only possible strategy so you may have to listen to one more bore's recollections and reflections on what seemed to him significant influences on erratic attempts at real human living in body and spirit.

The reality of people and the risks
'Getting real', as you might advise your parents, has been a life-long struggle of coming to terms with the reality of people, from parents and siblings to schoolmates and colleagues to beloved friends and persistent enemies or at least opponents. In all their different and often ambiguous ways they teach you about life in the Spirit. In the cherished memories life-story is love-story. People one has loved and loves, people who have loved and who still love one in spite of all, are primary sources of whatever we mean by spiritual life. This is certainly true for those who try to follow Jesus' example and command. Your baptism proclaimed as much: you are born and then reborn to a life of love by water and the Holy Spirit. We are able to love in that we are first loved, immediately by family and friends, ultimately by that great spiritual reality, the God who in New Testament terms is love.

The spiritual life then is a life of loving and of being loved and the historical sources are people, rooted for Christians in the tri-personal God of baptism, of Father, Son and Holy Spirit. (The sexist resonance of this language is bound to be a bit off-putting. One of the tasks for your generation will be to get beyond it.)

Of course people and loving are not problem-free. Ambiguities abound. Destruction threatens as fulfilment is promised. Betrayal shadows fidelity. Best friends may become worst enemies. Fratricide has a depressing history and civil war is reputedly the most savage.

The risks of people and of loving are only too real and too often issue in destruction for them to be ignored. They have to be integrated into the deeper life of the Spirit, the loving, forgiving re-creative life by which such betrayal and destruction may be overcome. By which they were overcome in Jesus. By which they could be overcome by his followers if they were not so inclined to follow their fearful and vengeful instincts. Baptism by water and the Holy Spirit has a transforming, recreating and loving potential in human life and love – that is why it is spoken of in terms of overcoming 'original sin', the fearful and vengeful instincts carried by the human community. It is not only the baptised, and certainly not always the baptised, who manifest this transforming potential. Baptism is its symbol. Loving and forgiving people are its realisation. The forgiving response in the famous example of Gordon Wilson and of many others less famous, remains a true source of spiritual living and loving.

Compassion and its causes

The spiritual is not just discernible in the personal-relational, central as that is. It emerges also in the larger commitments which people undertake for the sake of particular groups of people and communities. It inspires devotion to causes from caring for the sick and the poor to saving the earth, the community of all the living. Truth and beauty, freedom, justice and peace are typical of generic categories of the causes which inspire human, spiritual commitment. In reducing mood once more I will focus on compassion and the kinds of causes it generates.

Compassion, basically suffering with, enables one to share the human sufferings and privation which are such a prominent and continuing feature of our world. 'The whole earth is our hospital' in Eliot's words and compassion is essential to its healing. Healing comes from within person and community. Compassion is the *cead isteach*, the permission to enter.

In the Christian tradition, that permission was sought by God from Mary and by Jesus from the excluded and deprived with whom he would establish his new *koinonia*, the new healed and healing human community.

The several causes of a single lifetime prove nourishing and

frustrating. The wounded healer is frequently healed but incurs
new wounds also. Causes enlarge, energise and renew. They can
also delude, deceive and sometimes destroy. The free commitment to the great causes can become imprisoning obsessions in
which people, the usual origin and test of the cause, are obscured and even abused. Great causes, religious and political,
necessary as they are to humanity's breathing of the Spirit, must
at best endure partial failure. At worst, they may destroy the
causes' promoters and their would-be beneficiaries. This century,
even this short lifetime, has seen some horrific examples of causes
going wrong. That is why causes always need compassion just
as compassion, to be widely effective, must organise itself about
particular causes: fighting famine, promoting peace, preventing
HIV/AIDS at particular times in particular places for very particular people.

Creations and discoveries
The human spirit is restless in search of new developments, new
expressions, new discoveries. Artistic creation and scientific discovery bear witness to the reach of that restless spirit. For the
less gifted in those areas, the observers, readers and learners
rather than the creators and discoverers, entering into the works
of the gifted, or better, allowing these works to enter into them,
has its own transforming, liberating and healing effects. One's
spirit, oneself is set free, renewed and healed. In the present
high-energy state of artistic Ireland, despite its variable standards and inevitable pretensions, the spiritual possibilities are
many. Creativity carries its ambiguities but as a state of mind
encourages us beyond ourselves even if we then fall flat on our
faces. The risks of creating haunt every artist even as they haunted
Eliot's 'ruined millionaire' who endowed the earth. Self-exposure into self-transcendence would be apt summary of human
and divine creation in which we all share in some limited fashion. It characterises life in the spirit at so many levels from love
and friendship to the greatest artistic achievement.

Haunted by words as we are, it is exhilarating to find, to realise that 'finding' and 'discovery' have a Latin equivalent, *invenire*,
which issues in our word for inventing and making (creating).
The thrills of discovery which the great scientists (and archaeol-
ogists and explorers) enjoy are open to their students and followers.
In our world where such work has been seen as so different from

that of the artists, it is important to stress the imaginative leaps in scientific discovery and inventing and the discovering, coming-upon dimension of artistic achievement. What Richard Wilbur described as letting a poem happen to him reflects the giftedness which many poets and scientists, politicians and religious people experience in their best endeavours, their most spiritual activities.

On the threshold of contemplation

Faced with the given and the gift, finding a way to understand and express it, the spiritual in us may pause to rest in the gift and in achievement of understanding and expressing. For the restless human spirit in a distracted world, the resting is not easy. At its deepest that rest is silence and demands silence. And silence is risky, too risky for most of us most of the time and so we rush back to noisy thinking and talking and acting. Yet the people and the causes, the poems and the paintings and the scientific discoveries, summon us at times to silence. Not least the silence of awe and wonder at 'the achieve of, the mastery of the thing'. In a lifetime of gratitude and regrets, one of the most serious regrets is the repeated hesitancy on the edge of silence, on the threshold of contemplation. Perhaps your generation, Sarah, maturing through and beyond the distractions of the age, may find the courage and the skills to cross that threshold.

The risk of God

Crossing the threshold poses particular threats for would-be Christians. It involves the risk of God. Institutionalised and domesticated, ritualised and even sacramentalised, God remains mainly undisturbing, unchallenging. The comfort-blanket God providing irrational therapy for those who refuse to grow up is a common enough distortion. The real God of creation and incarnation, of crucifixion and resurrection is seldom risked.

The self-exposure involved seems too painful and fruitless to boot. The promised self-transcendence no longer sounds persuasive. And yet all the other self-exposures addressed here, from love and friendship through compassion and its causes to creation and discovery, hold a promise that incites trust that is of course sometimes betrayed but not always and not forever.

In later years I have become more conscious of our need to risk God, to follow the line of self-exposure into self-transcendence, or more accurately self-surrender. Human experiences have encouraged this mood and move. More recently a growing sense of the risks taken by the originator ('the ruined million-aire') in creating, in entering into compassionate companionship with the earth and its peoples, has driven me to risk a little more of myself in the silence and the darkness so well described in the spiritual and mystical traditions.

If you ever get this far, Sarah, you will undoubtedly be for-giving of an older man's ramblings and vague memories. Too vague indeed for the more concrete illustrations of a life-story that makes a botched love-story in search of a healing ending.

Slán agus beannacht,
Enda

CHAPTER TWENTY-ONE

Grace before Seventy

To anticipate by even one hour may prove presumptuous, like saying the grace and finding there is no meal; a too common contemporary experience. Reaching the biblical three score and ten is no more to be taken for granted than the next crossing of the road. The road may be the most obvious hazard as tiger-filled tanks race to the next growth point of the national economy. The heart and the head, all the war-weary organs, carry their own inbuilt and often undetected hazards. The second childishness of Shakespeare's seventh age may still be kept at bay but the 'lean and slippered pantaloon; ... with spectacles on nose' must struggle with 'a world too wide/ For his shrunk shank'. The fears are prudent but should not be paralysing. There is no sense yet of 'a tattered coat upon a stick'. And although the funerals of contemporary family and friends multiply, the call to grace and gratitude for them and all life's other gifts subtly merges with the need to give thanks for what we are about to receive, whatever that may be.

Identifying the lifelong child
Remembering in religious and secular ritual is about giving thanks, from Holy Week ceremonies to Arbour Hill to Remembrance Sunday. The eucharist provides for Christians the model supreme of remembering and giving thanks, of giving thanks through remembering. For this individual these communal celebrations, religious and secular, structure and renew his sense of who he is. They mark more or less deeply and sometimes permanently his public identity as Irish and Catholic, academic and priest and whatever. That public identity influences but does not determine his full personal identity, with its many historical twists and turns, its many private loves and hates, hurts and healings. Individual identity is a history beyond remembering in all its details, while one is still attempting to integrate even the forgotten details into a coherently responding and responsible person.

Responding and responsible persons are always incomplete. Their identity remains unfinished, an occasion for hope or despair, an opportunity for salvation or destruction. Final human and Christian identity remains at risk, even if the fires of earlier drama seem irreversibly banked. Death-bed conversions there still may be but they are no longer so obvious or notorious.

At this personally grace-filled time, the remembering and the thanksgiving focus first of all on a childhood which survived its own traumas, and those of later development, to form a permanent part of the present grimy adult. Of course it is the open, trusting, receptive attitude of that child that one is proud to observe still at work, despite the disappointments and disillusionments of the decades. It is more difficult to acknowledge the self-centred, demanding and resentful Döppelganger who hasn't gone away. Their coexistence and power struggles could be depressing and paralysing without the liberating gift of that other level of childhood which was revealed through baptism and nurtured through the community of Word and Sacrament, that of child of God. An arrogant, even ludicrous claim in a society which finds most God-talk embarrassing, and in a church whose mistreatment of children is so frequently in the headlines. And yet a radical affirmation of the ineradicable human dignity of everybody and a guarantee of the continuing significance of this ageing somebody. But how to attest and explain all that – there's the problem.

In classical theological terms, by faith and baptism we share Jesus' sonship of God. For those of us trebly schooled in that language it is difficult to keep in mind how opaque, if not meaningless, it has become to so many of the baptised, even to some of our own contemporaries. What a grace before seventy it would be to be able to unlock that language for friends, colleagues and students and release its liberating energies. Fumbling with rusty keys in unsteady hands will scarcely suffice.

Losing the biblical plot
Despite the inspiration of Vatican II and continuing systematic efforts in school and study group to implement it, the bible remains a largely foreign book to Irish Catholics. In the wider secular society to which Ireland belongs, and in its English language areas which were traditionally Protestant and biblical, the recent move by London's National Gallery to seek to educate the

new generation of art-lovers in the biblical basics of so much of
the greatest European art indicates a more profound and extensive vacuum. The annunciation and nativity stories and the
gospel accounts of the baptism of Jesus by John, all vividly told
and apparently self-explanatory and all subjects for major artists
in the past, may retain much of their aesthetic appeal without revealing the real significance of Jesus for the artist, for Jesus' followers and indeed for all humankind. If this man, conceived by
the Holy Spirit, born of Mary and baptised by John, proved to be
indeed the Son of God with whom the divine Father was well
pleased and through whom all human beings are called to be
children of God, the continuing child in each of us, Döppelganger and all, enjoys the dignity and support of being unconditionally and unfailingly loved. If we had some sense of our and
others' need for unconditional and unfailing love, and any sense
of its presence, we could read the biblical stories with a fresh eye
and a more understanding heart. In the last days before seventy,
the need is more evident. And even if the personal sense of loving presence remains fitful, the (ir)regular round of ritual, prayer
and people sustains the wayward child. 'How but in custom and
ceremony / Are innocence and beauty reborn.'

Presence and its terrors
Sensing this loving presence can be both terrifying and transforming. It can be terrifying as the abyss, the nothingness beneath, seems the more immediate prospect. Only as one becomes
aware of the abyss does one become aware of the presence creating, sustaining, prevailing. But the terror could still persist so
one is readily attracted to avoiding such encounters. In younger
and busier days, good works could offer guilt-free avoidance
while other distractions dissolved the terror at least temporarily.
But it is through the terror that one must finally go in search of
the presence. The risk of not coming through, of not finding, intensifies the initial fear. The risk of finding can have its own
terrors. The promise of finding, the promise of presence is the
promise of transformation, of conversion which has its destructive and frightening sides. Unless a seed fall into the ground.
Unless you take up your cross. Only he who loses his life will
save it. The possibilities are all about us always. Only occasionally under the pressure, under the grace of crisis or illness or
ageing, do we advert to them. More occasionally still do we realise, make actual, such possibilities.

Transformation does not come easily or often. And it always needs to be repeated. Conversion to the presence is a lifelong call and it seldom happens without its moments of terror. The security of the child of God is received and achieved along the way of the cross, the way of love and of life, a more transparent and so a more frightening prescription at seventy than at twenty when one felt naïvely ready to die for all kinds of causes.

The intervening fifty years have witnessed a rather fitful exploration of that twenty year old's early glimpse of an inspiring, judging and forgiving Father. Becoming a child of God is at once being and becoming, gift and task, a creative gift of the divine spirit and a slow and painful process of creative reception by the human spirit. In the parable of the Prodigal Son/Forgiving Father, as in the insight of Alcoholics Anonymous, hitting rock-bottom provides the moment of recognition. 'I will arise and go to my Father.' Few of us have such dramatic experiences. And even in our dark times the Father God of Jesus Christ is not automatically available or automatically consoling. The parables and the titles and the human analogies for all their potential riches do not guarantee breakthrough. Without an alternative human support system the child of God may be just a lost soul. With a strong human support system the fatherhood of God may appear irrelevant. How human support/community mediates God's presence will be addressed presently. Midst community or in solitude the individual must wrestle with the obscurities of child of God/fatherhood of God.

Gender has complicated the difficulties in recent decades. Even understood to be beyond gender and other human specifics, the constant reference to God as Father and the invariable use of the pronoun 'he' influenced profoundly most people's image and concept of God. The male resonances of such language affected community structures and practices, including prayer practices, in ways only now becoming obvious to us. When we have grown used to speaking of the Mother-God as easily as we speak of the Father-God we will have recovered a latent biblical dimension, found deeper human analogies for the unconditional divine love and opened the way to a more balanced understanding of child of God. But we will not have disposed of the mystery and its attendant obscurities.

The Hebrew scriptures do not neglect the tender, compassionate, loving God, the Father of his people (and eventually of all peoples). Yet the dominant impression is of a powerful and often fearsome God who punishes as well as liberates that people. The New Testament stress is quite different. The unknown carpenter from Nazareth is described as God's beloved son and Jesus dares to address the almighty creator and Lord of Israel as 'Abba'. The significance of the Abba move is not that of reinforcing gender distinction but of establishing intimacy in a tender and trusting relationship as much or more characteristic of mother-child relationship than of father-child. That parent-child intimacy becomes our inheritance by adoption in the Spirit, whereby we too say Abba.

Between mysteries or machines

Addressing the mystery as Abba is the work of the Spirit of baptism, the transforming and healing work of God. That is our work, the people's work, liturgy, in so far as we allow ourselves to be opened by the mystery of God within to the mystery without. We live between the mysteries. The sense of 'between' can sharpen with ageing. The experience of living between mysteries emerges in the interchange between the self and the other, human, natural and ultimate or divine.

Of course the sense of mystery is readily overlaid with self-indulgence and self-protection. Fear of the mystery and of the abyss surrounding it leads to the building of devotional, intellectual or other ramparts, which we never entirely escape or demolish. The true mystery of God within us and outside us, mediated incarnationally by Jesus, breached these ramparts and enables us to say Abba and to be one of the company of the sisters and brothers of Jesus. It is that mystery which finally prevails. As we seek to live with it, so we hope to die into it. Trust and truth, like the fire and the rose, will be finally one.

Living between the mysteries of before and after the historical self, of within and without the individual self, is always stressful and sometimes fragmenting. As we relax into the rhythm of time, the shelter of the living body and earth and the support of community, we may occasionally sense the mysterious creative and loving power that draws the fragments together and holds them in the hollow of the divine hand.

Stress and fragmentation have increased with the communications explosion and the apparent arrival of the global village. No place is safe from the distracting intrusions of the mobile phone. Information beyond management or need pours through the e-mailbox. The Internet lurks in wait for its latest addict. The enormous added value these developments can offer in almost every sphere of life, including prayer (cf the Irish Jesuits' prayer-site on the Internet, Sacred Space) is undeniable. Yet the sheer volume of interactions to which so many people are exposed nowadays and the trivial nature, yet addictive quality of so many of these interactions, make life very stressful when not utterly fragmenting. This may be more true of would-be septuagenarians as they face such developments so late in life. No doubt would-be twenty- and thirty-year olds find them no more distracting than their parents found the old-fashioned telephone and talk-radio. And children younger still seem to experience computers as a more natural extension of their fingers and minds than much earlier generations experienced the quill or even the biro. Immunisation against the feared excesses of the IT world in trivialisation and fragmentation may well come with early exposure. But will the dominance of machines affect the mediation of the mysteries? Will we live between machines and mechanical products rather than between mysteries, human, natural and divine? The same questions probably occurred to Gutenberg's contemporaries and perhaps to the witnesses of the earliest halting scripts. The current range and rate of change make such historical comparisons of limited value except to indicate that humanity is always having to save its human skin and dignity, and so its mysterious depths, from the negative effects of some products of its rampaging intelligence. In the present instance, those offering and receiving grace before thirty should have far more opportunity and responsibility for the saving than someone at grace before seventy.

Rest before seventy

Age is no more a guarantee of wisdom than youth is of idealism. Yet one might expect the struggles over the decades to have left some liberating sense of perspective and proportion whereby the trivia may be discounted and the really significant recognised and cherished. Or are the pace of change and the flood of information too great to allow any even provisional winnowing of that kind? Have the rat-tat-tat of the machines and the unceasing flux of images made attention impossible and dissolved real presences, human and divine? The answer to these and similar

questions is, 'not quite'. Without any pretensions to the role of
saoi at seventy, one can still find rest and renewal midst the hur-
rying chase of modern living. In his great faith poem, 'The
Pulley', George Herbert elaborates on a theme of St Augustine's
about the restless human heart finding its rest only in God:

When God at first made man,
Having a glasse of blessings standing by;
Let us (said he) poure on him all we can:
Let the world's riches, which dispersed lie,
Contract into a span.

So strength first made a way,
Then beauty flows, then wisdome, honour, pleasure;
When almost all was out, God made a stay,
Perceiving that alone of all his treasure
Rest in the bottom lay.

For if I should (said he)
Bestow this jewel also on my creature
He would adore my gifts instead of me,
And rest in Nature, not the God of Nature,
So both would losers be.

Yet let him keep the rest,
But keep them with such repining restlessnesse:
Let him be rich and wearie, that at least,
If goodnesse lead him not, yet wearinesse
May tosse him to my breast.

In his brilliant analysis of the poetic skill and power of this
poem, Seamus Heaney in *The Redress of Poetry*, speaks of how 'a
pun on the word "rest" is executed in slow motion', and how 'At
the end equilibrium has been restored to the system, both by the
argument and by the rhythm and rhyme, as "rest" and "breast"
come together in gratifying closure' (p 11). The argument, the
rhythm and the rhyme of a life move together if not quite towards closure, at times to gratifying rest in these later years. Just
when the pattern of regular sleep seems shattered for ever, a
resting in living and waking can overcome the 'repining restlessnesse' by some sense of being tossed on to the divine breast.
What had been too often the small and dark hours of unbelief
may become hours of grace-filled repose, in the interval between

the acts of a demanding drama, a lifelong mystery play. Interval reflections grow mellower. The drama is acquiring more shape, the mystery more meaning, the night less terror. Sometimes. The sleeplessness of dread from an earlier time yields to a more peaceful feeling of presence. Sometimes. The rest is, in Herbert's image, breast rest. Sometimes. To invoke Herbert once more, beyond the earlier stage 'more fierce and wilde / ... / Methought I heard one calling, Childe: / And I reply'd, My Lord'. Sometimes.

Upper room; community room; waiting room
Being an only child of God would be too much for a mere human being, rather like being the only conscious creature in an empty universe. The creation and Jesus stories finally come together in his being raised by the Spirit to be manifested as Son of God and as the firstborn of the new creation and the new humanity. By baptism in the same Spirit, the brothers and sisters of Jesus the Christ form the sacrament of the new human community, indeed of the new creation. In that transformed community, human and cosmic, loneliness is no longer insuperable. Community is a human possibility as well as a divine reality and divine gift. *Waiting for Godot* is no longer tragedy or farce. Estragon and Vladimir are not in some nameless place just passing time that will pass anyway. Time and place are the context of true community, with God already in attendance.

Even at seventy that faith-assertion remains fragile, vulnerable to the moods and tensions of daily living. Without the companionship of the brothers and sisters, the communal bread-baking and bread-breaking, faith would be unsustainable. The least ones, the hungry and thirsty, the sick and the homeless are the privileged brothers and sisters, most powerfully and immediately manifesting divine presence, divine call and human, holy communion. Central to community-communion is reception of the other(s), permitting them to enter one's house, one's mind, one's heart. It is to be inhabited by the others and to inhabit them in turn. The central Christian sacrament signifies that we are inhabited by Christ while we also inhabit him. But the Body of Christ comprises all the baptised, in principle all the redeemed, meaning my neighbour who is 'all mankind'. Being inhabited by an other comes at a cost. Host is also victim; there is sacrifice involved. Communion is truly transforming but at times crucifying. Cheap love and cheap grace have no part in Christian living.

The host-victim is primarily, however, a celebratory figure and a party-giver. Rejoicing in and with the others beyond the inevitable sorrows is the name of the Christian game. The dance of the Trinity, as some early theologians imagined it, offers a striking insight into the joyful communion into which the God of Jesus Christ has invited humankind.

Company: A retrospective

The picture gallery of the seven decades enjoys none of the framed reminders of his friends which Yeats enjoyed on his visit to the Municipal, now the Hugh Lane, Gallery. The company kept and lost to death were not likely to attract the eye of the portrait painter. Photographs, mainly snaps, lie around neglected. Memory and the mind's eye and ear form the gallery for any retrospective of those with whom in succeeding decades the bonds of friendship were dissolved in dying. Grandparents barely remembered, parents still painfully recalled, aunts, uncles, cousins, school and college friends, colleagues and neighbours, even enemies (if life is interesting enough one deserves a couple of enemies); they all form part of the shaping and the bonding, all leaving their indelible traces. Everybody's glory is that they had such friends. Christian glory includes them not only in retrospect but in prospect, a prospect that does not immediately ease the pain of separation. Retrospection is still necessary for that. The retrospective exhibition is for private viewing only. Other friends may share part of it but in the long reaches of the night when it is most likely to appear, the memorial gallery is a lonely but no longer a joyless place. The picture of a lost friend has, for all its flickering, a roundedness and a richness unavailable in the pressure of a living relationship. While all memories fade, the good ones are more durable and restorative. In the retrospective of a good night the grace before seventy is truly gracious. The company of the loved and loving dead proves communicative and convivial.

The gallery of the departed is also a gallery of their departing, full of installation works rehearsing the words and music, the rites and symbols with the distressful grieving at a particular tragic dying, the near celebratory grieving at the peaceful passing of a life clearly and effectively completed, and with the rich range of dying and grieving in between. The priest without a regular parish base has to face much fewer of these occasions but the ones he usually faces, of family and particular friends, can be both harrowing and exhausting. It is through the pain of the occasion that family member or friend finally and permanently inhabit him, and his grieving companions enter more fully into his further shaping.

In the years which follow, the night gallery is illumined by the day gallery of so many surviving friends and friends of friends. As if echoing Jesus' dying wishes, the experience of sharing the death and burial of a friend comes to light and to life in fresh life-giving bonds. The gallery of the dead nourishes the gallery of the living. In the approach to seventy, mutual enrichment between the galleries becomes more evident, if in many deeper losses only slowly and painfully so. At the far reach of Christian symbolism we know that we all die that others may have life. In one of the final acts of his life just before his tragic death, Jonathan Philbin Bowman recorded a series of 'thoughts for the day'. In one he defended human freedom in the most extreme circumstances. Even as one is being nailed to the cross one is still free to forgive one's crucifiers and refuse the category of resentful victim. It might have been his epitaph, all our epitaphs, if we learn how to die for others into the completion and transformation of life.

Living to be done and miles to go before we sleep – maybe
The prospect of death can become paralysing before its time, even if its time should turn out to be tomorrow. The retreat-master's story of the saint engaged in playing billiards who was asked what he would do if he were told he was to die tomorrow and replied 'I would finish the game', had a youthful appeal that still impresses. Sitting down and waiting to die is no substitute for the life that can still be lived and no preparation for the death that is somewhere along the road. Increasingly suspicious of one's temptation to self-importance in one's views and activities, one may develop a fresh freedom and renewed vision where the achievements may be limited but which still make room for the younger and more energetic to realise the values of God's reign in a society and church which have seriously lost their way.

The aged and unwaged, free of the burdens of paid work, have a final double responsibility: to the past and to the future. To the past they have the responsibility of evaluating the successes and failures in which they participated or which they at least closely observed. For example, the superficial dismissals or endorsements of the fifties in Ireland by 'liberals' or 'conservatives' restrict everybody's capacity to learn from the past and to plan for the future. Judicious critique of the past is essential to confident embrace of the future. The aged may sometimes have the resources to do it. A roster of people throughout the country who have lived and loved, achieved and failed thoughtfully and critically, could still be wisdom winnowers in a distracted and often unthinking society. The room for fresh energy and fresh ideas which their continuing contribution to church and society could make is still important. Room, space, freedom for the fresh, energetic and creative is what we need. The resourceful young and younger people are there; they are always there. Will the ethos of clerical preservation in church and of commercial accumulation in society continue to stifle them? At least let the oldies do their bit to set the young 'uns free. If that is what the young 'uns were about to receive, seventy would be magic, God-given magic.

The baptismal promise of new creation already requires that we be buried with Jesus Christ that we may rise with him to the fullness of life. That baptismal process is completed only in death. Will one be able to say grace as one is about to receive that final call and gift? For now one can only trust in the gracious caller and giver.